TEN PILLARS FOR AN *Amazing* MARRIAGE

Roderick Aguillard

FIRST EDITION

ISBN: 978-0-9974942-9-7

Library of Congress Control Number: 2016944163

Published by

Certa Publishing

P.O. Box 2839, Apopka, FL 32704

Printed in the United States of America

Foreword

The year was 1968. At the young age of twenty-eight my life was literally falling apart. On the surface it looked good. I was one of the youngest production supervisors working for Air Products and Chemical Company of East New Orleans. Married to a vivacious wife with two wonderful children.

From 1958 until 1968, I had been living in the fast lane of the night life: drinking, carousing and gambling. My last night out was at a Go-Go joint in East New Orleans. Near daylight, I was driven and dropped home in a drunken state.

The Bible is true, sin has a payday. Sin will cost you more than you want to pay! My physical body was depleted by alcohol, smoking and the night life. My finances were broken. My marriage was in shambles! Following the Go-Go joint escapade, and in the misery of my selfish sin, I repented in a bathtub and got born again.

In the spring of 1968, the alcohol consumption ended. The Go-Go joint visits were history. The gambling stopped.

All because I became a new creation in Christ Jesus! My marriage had a new beginning as the Holy Spirit restored the years the enemy had stolen. The Lordship of Jesus became the foundation of the Aguillard household and the foundation for a happy marriage.

In March of 2016, Marvelous Mary and I celebrated fifty-seven years of covenant relationship. Since 1968, we discovered ten pillars for building a strong and successful marriage. In the midst of many storms and setbacks, these ten pillars have helped us to stay the course in our relationship and have helped us to deepen our love for each other.

Please read this book slowly. Learn from our mistakes. Laugh at our conflicts. Rejoice in our victories. Glean from our wisdom. See the power of His grace and truth for a happy marriage.

We love all of you,

Rod & Marvelous Mary

Table of Contents

Chapter One

The Pillar of Communication

"Can two people walk together without agreeing on the direction?" (Amos 3:3 NLT)

Dr. James Dobson has a three-fold prescription for a successful marriage. **First and foremost is a common devotion to Jesus**. As a husband, the more I commune vertically with the Holy Spirit, the better I relate horizontally to my wife. Vice versa, my wife is at the feet of Jesus every morning. As she absorbs His divine grace, her relationship with me grows deeper and deeper.

Secondly, **a mutual commitment to covenant**. Marriage is a covenant, a merger of two lives, two wills, and two spirits until death parts. In covenant, there are no bail outs through the storms of life. In covenant, you are together for better or for worse. Covenant commitment is the glue that keeps a couple together through the disappointments, disagreements, setbacks, and heartbreaks of life.

The third key to a healthy and happy marriage is **good**

communication. Marvelous Mary, my wife of fifty-seven years, is a great communicator. She is full of life, joy, and words. The social experts claim that the average woman has 24,000 words a day. I once heard a testimony that a newly married man had not spoken to his wife in six months. When asked why, he said, “I didn’t want to interrupt her!” I assume this was not a real relationship but it is amusing when you think of 24,000 words a day.

Communication is the art of sharing your life; being an open book especially in your marriage relationship. In open communication, a couple learns to walk together. Marriage is like a highway. It is full of forks and four way stop signs. The marriage highway is full of bumps and curves. In reality, marriage is a life time of merging, of becoming one in thought and action.

The root word of communication is to commune. Commune is to hold or to share intimate conversation; heart to heart sharing. (Webster’s) Communication is much more than facts, comments, nods or grunts. Healthy communication in marriage is the sharing of life: feelings, fears, failures, frustrations, and future. Marvelous Mary and I have been through enough storms to sink five Titanic’s. But through the storms and setbacks, we have always communicated, and we shared our tears, and merged in the grace of God. Through it all, we learned to trust Him and our love for each other grew deep and rich. I want to share a powerful word of God in regards to healthy communication:

"A word aptly spoken is like apples of gold in settings of silver." (Proverbs 25:11)

Let's look at the five apples of gold in communications for a happy marriage:

The First Golden Apple of Communication:

In disagreements, a woman's line of logical thoughts is totally different from a man's. Therefore men, we need to be patient, calm and ask the Lord to understand our wives make-up and pattern of behavior. For example, my wife is a TJ Maxx shopper and she is thrilled by her great discount buys. Two or three years ago my wife got a TJ Maxx credit card. After one month, I received a TJ Maxx credit card bill for over $200. I overlooked it until there was another $200 plus credit card bill. At that point, I asked her for an explanation. She said that whenever she bought over $200 on the TJ Maxx credit card they sent her a $10 discount coupon for her next purchase. My response, "I will give you $10 a month. No more TJ Maxx credit card. Rather, use Sam's Discover Card, two percent cash back." She had an emotional reaction, "You spend more money on hunting and fishing." Again, I said, "No TJ Maxx credit card, Sam's Discover Card, two percent cash back." Then another emotional response, "You send all your daughters money on Valentine's Day, Mother's Day, and Christmas!" Again, "No TJ Maxx credit card, Sam's Discover Card, two percent cash back." One final resistance, "Ok, I will get a job at Walmart to cover it." With authority, "No

TJ Maxx credit card, Sam's Discover card, two percent cash back." A sheet of ice fell in the room as my clear and concise communication won the day. I rejoice in her obedience! It has been over three years now and she uses the Sam's credit card, two percent cash back. In communication, I have heard that a wife's brain is wired differently. Below is a picture description of the female and male brain. I do not know where I discovered these two diagrams so I changed some of the details not to violate any copy rights.

THE MALE BRAIN - ELEVEN

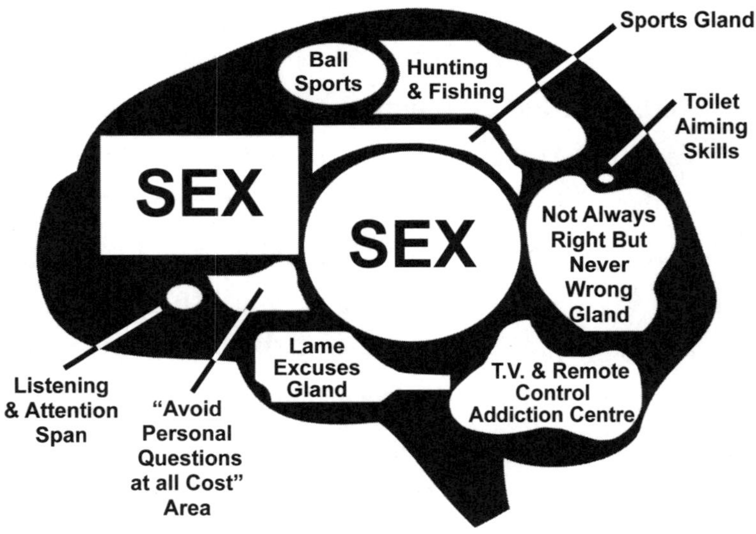

FOOTNOTE: *The "listening to children cry in the middle of the night" gland is not shown due to it's small and underdeveloped nature. Best viewed under a microscope.*

THE FEMALE BRAIN - TEN

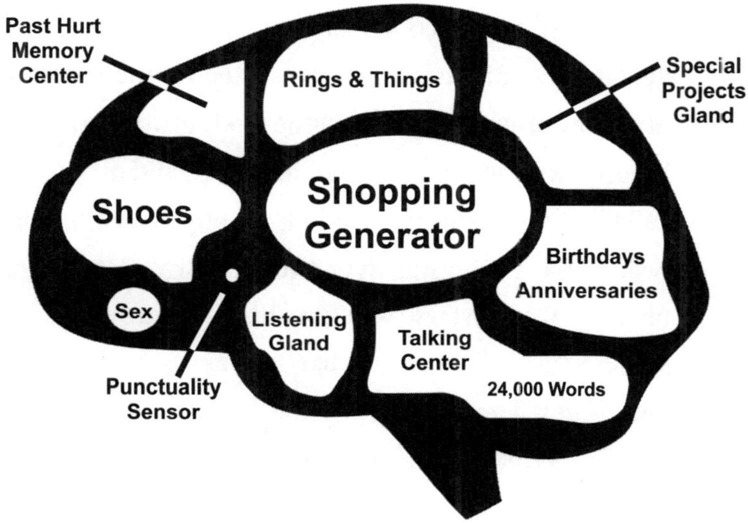

FOOTNOTE: *Note how closely connected the small sex cell is to the listening gland.*

The Second Golden Apple of Communication:

In regards to issues, differences and major decisions, pick the right time and the right place to communicate.

> *"A time to rend, and a time to sew; a time to keep silence, and a time to speak."* (Ecclesiastes 3:7)

During our fifty-seven years of marriage, Mary and I have had numerous disagreements. As we have matured under the leadership of the Holy Spirit, we have learned the following principles of discussing differences until we come to an agreement.

1. We met in private, behind closed doors where the children could not hear us. (Children cannot handle

open arguments or disagreements between their parents.)

2. We usually discussed our disagreements and our decision making process in a relaxed moment without distractions such as: cell phones, television, etc.
3. Finally, we tried to work out our issues and differences calmly without anger. In our younger years, there was a major conflict over birth control. I was anti-birth control; Mary was pro-birth control. We had some anger and heated discussions over this issue. One night, I moved out of the bedroom. I thought I could manipulate her by this bold move which was not God. Manipulation is a form of witchcraft. Later, during the early night, I peeked in to see if she was weeping. Lo and behold, she was laying comfortable with a smile on her face. The next night, I moved back into the bedroom. Apparently, I had a preference; not a conviction.

In our continual conflict, we agreed to see a mediator to help us before our marriage went into a crisis. We met with my spiritual father, Pastor/Apostle Jim Clark. After hearing us out, he gave us two biblical solutions to choose from. First, to Mary, wives submit to your husbands. In other words, stop the birth control and have more babies. By the way, we already had five children. The second biblical choice was given to me. Honor the weaker vessel. Practice birth control. On the way home, my wife was steaming and said,

"Don't ever take me back to Jim Clark again!" She assumed I would stand on the first biblical solution, wives submit! At that moment, she didn't realize that I had taken the second alternative, "Honor the weaker vessel." Conflict was over with. No crisis. A home restored and united because we humbled ourselves and sought out wise counsel. You and yours may need to do the same.

The Third Golden Apple of Good Communication:

Realize the power of words and make sure to use the right words when you speak to your spouse. The power of words:

> *"Death and life are in the power of the tongue: and they that love it shall eat the fruit thereof."* (Proverbs 18:21)

I heard Kenneth Copeland state, "Words are containers, they either contain life or they contain death!" My words to Marvelous Mary (my wife) are either full of love and life or they are full of rejection and death. Often over the fifty plus years of our marriage I have spoken down to Mary. By grace, I have learned to repent and receive forgiveness. Today, my negative words are few and far apart.

Positive words build up.

> *"Pleasant words are as a honeycomb, sweet to the soul, and health to the bones."* (Proverbs 16:24)

All of us need praise and compliments. This is by divine design, it establishes our worth. Men, your wife will become what you feed her! You feed her words filled with honey; you will get honey! Read this testimony: Some brothers ganged up on their sister and told her she was skinny and ugly. The result was she had a low self-image; shy, rejected and withdrawn. Later she met a man by the name of John who fell in love with her. He kept telling her over and over again how she was charming and attractive. Eventually, the caterpillar came out of her cocoon and carried herself as a beautiful butterfly. Later John stated, "Look what I have done with my words." Positive words will build your wife. I have pet names for Mary that build! I call her Marvelous Mary; my woman, beautiful. There are certain word building names that she does not want me to share or write publically: Fox; Holy Hunk; Sexy. So I will honor her and not state them (smiling). I have pet names that I would like for her to say that would build my self-image: Big Daddy; Lover Boy; Tarzan; Lord with a little l. She refuses. So be it!

The wife will become the sum total of what the husband says to her and says about her.

> *"A wholesome tongue is a tree of life: but perverseness therein is a breach in the spirit."* (Proverbs 15:4)

Men, verbal abuse tears down, divides, and destroys. Verbal affirmation edifies and builds up. I watched it over the years in couples I tried to help. One lady was escorted to my office by one of her friends. Her eyes were actually glazed over because she was brutally abused by a husband's hateful words. My advice was separation or she would mentally lose her mind. At the same time when a wife talks back and lashes out at her husband in anger, she ministers disrespect and death. A husband's manhood is crippled when a wife talks down to him by calling him wimp or loser. Again, negative words carry rejection and death to a relationship.

The Fourth Golden Apple of Good Communication:

Gratitude. A constant flow of thanks to each other and for each one is "the oil" that "lubricates" the engine of a marriage. Every morning my wife tells me how much she loves me and appreciates me. The measure she measures out to me I measure back to her. It enlarges my heart to love and appreciate her.

As a spouse, every day at every opportunity verbalize gratitude and it will spark romance. It is so true,

> *"Death and life are in the power of the tongue..."* (Proverbs 18:21)
>
> *"A word fitly spoken is like apples of gold in settings of silver."* (Proverbs 25:11)

Again men, words of appreciation and gratitude carry life, and she does become what you feed her. So do it daily and on an often basis! Express gratitude and appreciation to your wife. Thank her for cooking. Tell her what a great mother she is. Admire and vocalize her beauty. When you are intimate with her, as you lay there, thank her for the pleasure she gave you. Give thanks for every deed or act. Make it your duty to affirm her. The spark and flow of romance is built on gratitude!

A great and healthy sex life does start in the kitchen and in the living room as you speak words of admiration and appreciation for her. Sexual intercourse is the ultimate communication and happens because of your positive words of affirmation. Murmuring, complaining and criticism kill romance. Murmuring is filled with rejection and death. Whether it be the husband or wife, complaining and criticism will eventually put a marriage into a crisis.

Question: Is there any atmosphere of gratitude in your home or is there an atmosphere of murmuring and aggravation? Men, do you create an atmosphere of demands and commands which will bring an oppression on your wife? Is this your attitude: "I am the head! I work hard! I provide! Therefore when I get home I expect a hot meal, hot coffee, hot lips and a hot wife." If so, your macho man approach just suppressed your wife and there is no fuel nor oil in the engine of romance. You can reverse this negative today! When you walk in from work, tell her how beautiful she is! Thank her for keeping the house clean and in order. Thank her for cooking and caring about you. Compliment her motherhood and the way she dresses. A few days and words of gratitude will lubricate the engine of marriage and spark the flames of romance. Men, you will have a tigress in your bedroom if you will merely adore your wife with words of thanksgiving and gratitude.

The Fifth Golden Apple of Communication:

"Esteem your relationship more than your issues" (Ron Corzine). "In matters of principle, stand like a rock. In matters of taste, swim with the current" (Thomas Jefferson). Husband…wife…be flexible. Most things are just not that important. It is not worth an unhealthy relationship. Esteeming your relationship is more valuable than your issues. I really do have numerous personal examples of this truth for a happy marriage. One is our pet dog's hair issue: one evening as I was watching the news in our den, I looked down on our dark wool rug and there was white dog hair spread out on surface. Hair of any kind tends to negate my food appetite. I called Marvelous Mary into the room and pointed to the dog hair. Jackie is a short haired Jack Russell with a coat of furry skin that is mostly white. Short haired dogs shed. My response in my lost appetite was "Mary, Jackie has to go! The original owner who gave it to us as a puppy will gladly take her back." She replied, "No, I am covenant with dogs!" My response, "I am not covenant with dogs, just with humans. Jackie has to go!" At this firm statement she began to cry. As the tears began to flow, I crushed her heart. Then in my low and confused state, the words of the great Bible teacher, Ron Corzine spoke to me from my spirit man, "esteem your relationship more than your issues!" At that very moment, the dog hair issue was dropped and as I write, Jackie is safely laying on a couch across from me shedding her white hair, and the iRobot Roomba automatic vacuum machine just went by my feet and onto a rug sucking up Jackie's white hair. Mary cared enough about my issue to buy a $259 machine to keep the house dog hair free!

Chapter Two

The Pillar of Listening

Hearing or listening is one of the most important words in the Bible. Our Lord's last instructions to the seven churches in Revelation was, "He that has an ear, let him hear what the Spirit says or is saying to the churches…" Hearing or listening is the most important factor of great communication for a healthy marriage. One of the greatest ways to love your wife is to listen to her with an intent to understand. Often I have shared, "A listener is a lover; a lover is a listener!" Since my new birth over forty-eight years ago, I have disciplined my mind and heart to be a good listener.

Listed are four benefits of listening:

1. **Listening shows respect**. When you don't pay attention to what others have to say, you send a message that you don't value them. When I am trying to communicate with another person and he looks away or interrupts, the conversation is over. Conversation that has value must be a

two-way street.

When you listen to your spouse or to others, you communicate respect and that you care about them. I was sitting next to a man by the name of Ron on a flight from Tampa, Florida to New Orleans. I began to ask him questions and he shared his life experiences as I intently listened. He was a prosperous owner of a water company. In his past, he fought as a mercenary soldier in Vietnam. He shared an episode where he was almost killed. He avoided death by hiding underneath a vehicle. While overseas, he divorced his wife and then married a native lady from Vietnam. He came home and started his water company. In the course of his life, he researched and practiced several religions: Catholicism, Buddhism, Hinduism, etc. In all of it, he has never found God. Having captured his heart through caring enough to listen, I shared my faith in Jesus Christ and gave him one of my books that I have written, *Going Through the Storms of Life*. Two or three weeks later, he wrote me a letter thanking me for the book and that it helped him in understanding who God is. I rejoiced! All because I cared enough to listen to him. "The first duty of love is to listen," (Paul Tillich). Men, do you want to have a great marriage? Do you want to have a wife that is deeply in love with you? Then, take time out to listen to her. A lover is a listener! And a listener receives love in return. Just do it!

2. **Listening builds relationships.** People who are self-focused mostly talk about themselves and show little

listening interest in others. They are self-centered and talk about their own concerns most of the time. In doing so, they rarely develop strong or lasting relationships with others. Everyone needs someone who he feels really listens to him! Being an avid listener is a key, if not the key in developing a healthy marriage or any lasting relationships with others.

Who is your best friend? Why is he or she your best friend? I can answer that for you. It is someone who knows you in communication by being a good listener. Several years ago I was in the cardio room of a local gym. A young man and lady were taking a lunch break together and were side by side on the treadmills. For over thirty minutes they were in a meaningful conversation, both good listeners. As I walked out, I spoke to the young lady who I knew at the reception desk. I asked her if she knew the couple on the treadmills. She said "Yes." Before she could say any more about them, I replied, "They are not married." She said, "You are right." "How did you know that?" They communicate too well with the other: it was a two way street of talking and listening. Healthy for a marriage; unhealthy for two married people that had found great communications outside their marriage. Are you getting the picture? Do you consider yourself to be an **avid listener** to your spouse?

3. **Listening builds loyalty**. If you and I don't practice listening to our spouse, they will find others who will. God created us to be loved through healthy communication.

As communication breaks down between husband and

wife, it causes ongoing marriage conflicts. If a conflict is not corrected through healthy communication, it could evolve into a crisis. A crisis often results in separation and possible divorce.

Any relationship that involves avid listening has long lasting loyalty. Everyone loves a good listener and draws to him or her. Covenant relationships, staying together for better or for worse, is built on the pillar of listening which results in a heart-felt loyalty.

4. **Listening generates insights, values, and ideas**. For example, Chili's Restaurants, according to Restaurants and Institutions Magazine, is one of the nation's best run food service chains. Almost eighty percent of its menu comes from the suggestions of unit managers.

Men, we learn our wife and we learn others by listening. We hear life by listening. We learn God by being still and listening to His voice through His written word.

In the sixth grade, I learned the following rhyme and it stayed with me. "There was a wise old owl who sat in a tree. The more he saw, the less he spoke. The less he spoke, the more he heard. Why can't we be like that old bird!" Help me Lord Jesus to lean into people and be a better listener. A listener is a lover; a lover is a listener.

Let's take a few minutes to develop your listening skills. I am not sure these thoughts are original. It is merely a common sense conclusion.

First, look at the listener. Give your spouse your undivided attention. Do not look off, put down the newspaper and put your cell phone on silent, focus on the other person! Give your spouse or whomever is talking eye contact. Love your spouse with our eyes and your ears.

Second, don't interrupt! This certainly makes anyone feel unloved and disrespected. By grace, relax your mind! Hold your peace! Don't wait for an opening to get your thoughts in, focus on what your wife or husband is saying. Let the other person finish talking.

I was visiting a pastor's home in Pennsylvania. The pastor had gathered his men leaders around me for questions and dialogue. My wife was sitting with the leader's spouses. I could hear the ladies talking and it was rapid fire. It sounded like a group of hens laying eggs and cackling as hens do when they are laying.

I questioned my wife, later. With so much talking and so little listening was anything accomplished? She claimed it went well. That response baffled me. Men can only hear and understand one statement at a time. Women tend to be multi-tasked and can hear many statements at one time and grasp some meaning from each.

Third, be a good listener, focus on understanding. Research has found that most people can only recall about fifty percent of what they hear immediately after they hear it. I know when I am hearing a gospel message being preached or taught I take detailed notes. Even as I do this, my recall within twenty four hours is very little. Some notes I keep to go over for recall and meditation. In this manner I can apply the truth received into my life which becomes wisdom to live by.

Eric Allenbaugh gives five guidelines for understanding as you listen:

- Listen with your eyes. Stay focused on the one sharing.
- Listen with a head/heart connection.
- Listen with empathy. Try to put yourself in their place or circumstance.
- Listen with the intent of understanding where the individual is coming from.
- Listen as you would like to be listeners of your thoughts. The law of love, "do unto others as you would have them do to you…"

Fourth, suspend your judgment! In other words, just wait and hear out the person. Be slow to speak. Let the person finish their thoughts before you respond. Be slow to judge where the individual is coming from as they communicate. Remember, there are no simple answers. God is simple, but human beings are complex. Your wife is a mystery. Her brain has logic but it is wired with a God designed emotional charge. She can think, feel, walk and talk all at the same time! Slow down. Suspend your logical judgments and listen intently to her deep desires or setbacks.

Fifth, ask questions for clarity: this takes patience and empathy. This is why I call a listener a lover. Gently ask follow up questions to seek clarity. I can recall one particular incident as I ministered to a pastor's wife. She was a frustrated mess and rambled as she talked of her dilemma. At some point during our sharing, I asked her a specific question: "What do you mean by that statement?" Her eyes brightened as she saw the source of her frustration or anxiety.

As you ask for clarity in a non-threatening way, people will realize that you really care. As a result, they will open up and tell you in detail their fears, their dreams and their disappointments. In fact, they will tell you their whole life story. I was flying to San Antonio, seated by Ralph, a seventy-four year old man that I met for the first time. I began to ask him questions about his life. He opened up and told me about his difficulties and disappointments. He had a triple heart bypass; he had the beginning of Parkinson's disease; he hated President Bush because his son was killed in Iraq. As I listened, I felt a burden of a defeated life. As we neared landing, I told him about my source of peace and joy through the Lord Jesus. His response, "I wish I could believe like you!" As we landed, I laid hands on him and prayed over him. Tears began to flow! God touched him, all because

I listened with compassion. In your marriage, please listen with compassion and understanding in regards to your husband or wife's fears, failures, ambitions and successes! It is certain, you will have a happy marriage. **A listener is a lover!**

Sixth, always make listening your priority, not your talking. Marvelous Mary and I traveled to San Antonio to spend the weekend with two pastor couples coming into the Network of Related Pastors. This is a group of pastors over which I am the Senior Overseer. We were at dinner in our first official meeting. My desire was to make listening a priority to learn from them and to see how we could help them to be successful pastors. I did not share that objective with my wife up front; so I take the blame for it not going in that direction. At this particular time, we were going through personal problems with a bipolar daughter separated from her husband and an older son with serious marriage problems. They inquired about our children. Three of my children were doing great but two were in a serious storm. She innocently and openly shared her burden, but it took up most of our conversation. Later, I tried to quietly correct her but it didn't go well. But in this lesson of communication, she learned to make listening a priority.

So in conclusion, for a healthy marriage and a healthy life with others, develop the skill of listening: listening to God, listening to those you love and listening to people. This will do much in the fulfillment of the great commandment,

> *"Jesus said unto him, Thou shalt love the Lord thy God with all thy heart, and with all thy soul, and with all thy mind. [38] This is the first and great commandment. [39] And the second is like unto it, Thou shalt love thy neighbour as thyself. [40] On these two commandments hang all the law and the prophets."* (Matthew 22:37-40)

A listener is a lover, a lover of God and a lover of people. *Have a happy and healthy marriage by being a good listener!*

Chapter Three

The Pillar of Covenant

The Kingdom of God is all about covenant relationships. When David became King over all of Israel, the scripture declared that all the elders meet with the King at Hebron and *"...King David made covenant with them..."* (II Samuel 5:3). He made a covenant. He made a declaration of a sacred and a life-long union. In 1968, I was born again. I was spiritually born into covenant with the Lord Jesus. In a moment of time, I became His son...His servant and His soldier. In covenant God writes His laws, His moral law upon our hearts:

> *"For this is the covenant that I will make with the house of Israel after those days, saith the Lord; I will put my laws into their mind, and write them in their hearts: and I will be to them a God, and they shall be to me a people."* (Hebrews 8:10)

In covenant, the great commandment is written upon our hearts,

"To love God with all our heart, soul and mind and to love our neighbor as ourselves." (Matthew 22:37-38)

And God's word declares that all the law and the prophets are fulfilled in these two commands. Therefore covenant is not a partnership: It is not a law/legal system but it is a merger; a divine union; a state of being one!

Again, referring to the covenant of King David and the tribes of Israel, David spoke covenant language "…we are your bone and your flesh…" We are integrated as one! "*Greater love hath no man than this, that a man lay down his life for his friends*" (John 15:13). This is a covenant statement.

During August of 2005, Hurricane Katrina devastated Southeast Louisiana which included New Orleans, St. Bernard, and Plaquemine's Parish. We, the Reserve Church Body, had the privilege of hosting the 82nd Airborne, the seasoned Black Hawk Helicopter Warriors of the Iraq War. There were approximately two hundred men and women. Some of the finest young people I have ever met. They were merged as a fighting unit. They were one in heart and mind. Their attitude was obedience no matter what the cost, a biblical picture of covenant. They were with us for ten days. On the Sunday that they were on our grounds, about one hundred attended the morning service. The Sunday morning tithes was given up front to ushers holding the offering buckets. Following the giving, the local church believers sat down. I looked to my right and the one hundred warriors were standing at attention as a unit waiting for my command to sit down. Covenant hearts under authority. I said, God, "Give me one hundred twenty believers like this and we will turn the world upside down." As we move into the end of the age, may the Holy Spirit separate to Himself an obedient Body of Covenant believers!

Marriage is a covenant! It is a merger of a man and a woman where they become one. One in spirit, soul, and body. An inseparable relationship that is bone of bone and flesh of flesh. A life- long committed relationship that vows to stay together until death parts. In my B.C. days, that is Before Christ, I was selfish and evil. As a married man, I would live in the lounges and night clubs leaving my wife at home. My dad would tell her to divorce me. Her response, "I am a Catholic and my church teaches no divorce." In this statement she was declaring that she was in a covenant marriage, a divine union with God and man.

Marriage is a covenant! It is not a me deal, it is a we deal. In marriage, we are in for the long haul. We may not always agree, but we will not forsake our covenant vows. As the body of Christ, we are in covenant with God and His people. It is a we deal.

> *"When one member suffers, we all suffer...when one member is honored, we all rejoice with him..."*
> (I Corinthians 12:26)

Listen to the covenant language of Isaiah 53:4.

"Surely he hath borne our griefs, and carried our sorrows: yet we did esteem him stricken, smitten of God, and afflicted."

He bore our sickness and took away our pains. Covenant is not a me deal, it is a we deal!

A few years back, Pastor Larry Stockstill of Bethany Church in Baton Rouge shared several attitudes of covenant relationships. I am going to take his main points and apply it to marriage.

Sacrifice: "I will live for you!" My life belongs to Jesus and to the Body of Christ and to Marvelous Mary. I lay down my life for my wife. What hurts her, hurts me. When she is happy I am happy; we are merged, we are one. Her burden is my burden. All that I am, all my resources, my talents, my time, and my finances are at her disposal. In covenant, I live to love and serve her. In your marriage, your husband or wife will have a burden, a weight that they cannot carry alone. In covenant, we yoke up together and carry it as one. Mary is my tomato stake that holds me up through the storms of our life and I am her tomato stake in the midst of setbacks. In December of 2008, my oldest daughter, Lynne Aguillard Venus tragically lost her life. Our local church body yoked up to us and together we went through a terrific storm and setback. This is the power of covenant connections: your burden is my burden.

A second principle of covenant relationship is **Surrender: I will learn about you!** Marvelous Mary and I have been married fifty-seven years as of this March 2016. Overall, it has been a wonderful journey in spite of disappointments and disagreements. Through it all, the bad times, the good times, the sad times and glad times, we have learned about each other. We know deeply each other's hearts, thoughts, ambitions and desires. I have been a student of Mary's behavior. Someone could come to me and say my wife was caught in a lie. My response, never. She is full of God's word and has impeccable integrity. Then another accusation, "She is not dependable or trustworthy." My response, "She is Mrs. Faithful." She is loyal to her God, her church, her husband and her family. And loyalty is royalty. In covenant, I have learned of her; I know her.

In a marriage covenant our statement to our spouse should be: **"I love you for who you are and not what you do for me!"** My relationship with Marvelous Mary is not based on her performance or how much she does for me. It is a blessing when she serves me, cooks for me, washes and dries my clothes, keeps our house clean and neat, and the list of her love actions goes on and on. Beyond all that she does, I love Marvelous Mary for who she is: kind, loyal, faithful, honest, longsuffering, joyful and pleasant, merciful, giving, and not a respecter of persons. Just as we praise God for who He is and we thank Him for what He does. In my covenant union and merger with Mary, I praise her for who she is and I thank her for what she does.

Are you getting the picture of covenant? Marriage is a covenant. One last quote from Pastor Stockstill, "**I give up**

my right to be right!" This is a powerful covenant attitude. My relationship to my wife is not based on our agreements or disagreements. If it would be, our marriage would be in a crisis because we are both strong leaders. I jokingly share with Mary, "I am not always right, but I am never wrong!" But we are in union. We are one. Neither one of us has to be right or win an argument to prove anything. We are not in a competition or in a debate. We are deeply in love and deeply committed to each other regardless of our different views or perspectives. How about you and yours?

Finally, **covenant is an undying faithfulness to a God-given relationship**. Fifty-seven years ago, Marvelous Mary was God's gift to me. She so completes me. We are so one! We both say to each other in our old age, "I can't live without you!"

Two concluding thoughts, God honors the marriage covenant of a man and a woman and He hates divorce. This scripture truth should put the fear of God into a believer who declares that Jesus is Lord.

> *"And this have ye done again, covering the altar of the LORD with tears, with weeping, and with crying out, insomuch that he regardeth not the offering any more, or receiveth it with good will at your hand. [14] Yet ye say, Wherefore? Because the LORD hath been witness between thee and the wife of thy youth,* ***against whom thou hast dealt treacherously: yet is she thy companion,***

*and **the wife of thy covenant**. [15] And did not he make one? Yet had he the residue of the spirit. And wherefore one? That he might seek a godly seed. Therefore take heed to your spirit, and let none deal **treacherously against the wife of his youth**. [16] For the LORD, the God of Israel, saith that he **hateth putting away**: for one covereth violence with his garment, saith the LORD of hosts: therefore take heed to your spirit, that ye deal not treacherously."* (Malachi 2:13-16)

God Hates Divorce! When divorce is rampant, it is an indication of a rebellious generation and a crumbling civilization. In 1930, married couples accounted for eighty-four percent of all households. In 2005, married couples accounted for 49.7 percent of all households. In Orleans Parish, married couples account for only 29.6 percent of all households. We need a Third Great Awakening. **God hates divorce** because it destroys the godly seed. I have an older son who divorced his first wife for another woman and a worldly lifestyle. It was an ugly divorce and my four grandchildren were utterly destroyed. A broken home, broken hearts, and broken lives. As I write, two of them are in drug rehabilitation. Wondering wanderers in their young twenties. Is there hope for the wounded and the victims of a tragic divorce? Yes, with God all things are possible. As grandparents, we are in the gap standing for their recovery and restoration.

In conclusion, the marriage law is written in our hearts,

"The wife is bound by the law as long as her husband liveth; but if her husband be dead, she is at liberty to be married to whom she will; only in the Lord." (I Corinthians 7:39)

Chapter Four

The Pillar of Forgiveness

In life's relationships, offenses are certain. In marriage, it is the merging of two wills and in the process offenses are certain.

> *"But whoso shall offend one of these little ones which believe in me, it were better for him that a millstone were hanged about his neck, and that he were drowned in the depth of the sea. [7] Woe unto the world because of offenses!"* (Matthew 18:6-7)

An offense is a stumbling block, a carefully laid trap. Webster's dictionary defines offense as an attack; a happening that often creates anger or resentment. Offense means to be hurt by someone's words or actions or just a lack of it.

In marriage, most conflicts have to do with a power struggle. "I'm right, you are wrong." "I want my way, you want your way." "Let's do this, let's not do this." Disagreements in the marriage are very common especially in the early years when the two wills are merging.

Since offenses are certain in close relationship. How do you deal with them? In the 1980's, I heard one well known teacher give this scenario of the wrong way to handle hurt or an offense:

1. If you focus on the offense,
2. If you rehearse it, play it over and over in your mind and build a case against the offender,
3. It will curse you, you will end up with a root of bitterness and torment will follow!

Rather than nurse and rehearse an offense or an angry disagreement, obey (Ephesians 4:26-27),

> *"Be ye angry, and sin not: let not the sun go down upon your wrath: [27] Neither give place to the devil."*

Do not give opportunity to the devil. Do not let an offense and unforgiveness give jurisdiction to the devil to divide your marriage or any close relationship. The truth is unresolved anger gives demonic powers arguments to war against your home. Marvelous Mary and I decided to have a home birth delivery for our fifth and last child. We were going to be assisted by two RN's and had a back-up doctor. The night before the delivery we had a heated disagreement, two egos at work. In our unresolved conflict, my wife stated that if we didn't settle the disagreement that we should not risk a home delivery because of the possible demonic intrusion over unresolved anger. I took heed, we repented and forgave each other. The next day in the quietness of our home, she gave birth to a beautiful eight and half pound baby girl. We named her Angelle Lea. Today she is a thirty-seven year old married mother with four children—a beauty on the inside and the outside, an Esther in the house. She was birthed by two forgiving parents.

The scripture declares that unresolved anger or bitterness is sinful and divisive. A marriage filled with anger, fussing and fighting will become self-destructive.

> *"But if ye have bitter envying and strife in your hearts, glory not, and lie not against the truth.*
> *15 This wisdom descendeth not from above, but is earthly, sensual, devilish."* (James 3:14-15)

God's remedy for offenses, hurts and anger is to simply forgive. A lady in our church called me late one night, and awakened me out of a deep sleep. Immediately she told me how her husband offended her and asked me what she should do. My response, "Forgive him!" She replied, "Oh, Okay that's what I will do." After that incident, my phone was disconnected at bedtime.

> *"Let all bitterness, and wrath, and anger, and clamour, and evil speaking, be put away from you, with all malice:*
> *32 And be ye kind one to another, tenderhearted, **forgiving one another**, even as God for Christ's sake hath forgiven you."* (Ephesians 4:31-32)

Verse thirty-two commands us to forgive one another even as God for Christ's sake has forgiven us. Forgiveness is the centerpiece of the cross. Often, in the morning during my communion time, I thank Him that my sins are forgiven. They are as far from me as the East is from the West. Rejoicing! The forgiven ought to live in a spirit of forgiveness.

Forgive means to simply **let it go**! Forgive, do not live in past offenses, hurts or disappointments. I have heard it said, "To have a healthy marriage, do not keep a scorecard!" As a pastor I have mediated marriage conflicts where at least one of the spouses kept a scorecard that went back years: "You did not do this!" "You wimped out on this decision!" On and on the accusations of a score card beat the husband or wife into a sense of failure and rejection. If you are going to have a happy marriage, you must throw away the scorecard. Do not keep a record of all past wrongs, hurts or inaction. Forgive! Let it go! Do not let the past hurts determine the future and the failure of your marriage.

Many years ago, I kept a scorecard on Eddie the Deacon. After I got born again at the age of twenty-eight, I attended a rural Baptist Church. In this particular local church there were open business meetings. Minor and major decisions were made by public discussion and followed by a congregational vote. It seemed to me that Eddie the Deacon always resisted the pastor and had open heated discussions opposing my pastor's vision request. My offense for my pastor and I kept a scorecard. Unresolved offense always results in anger and bitterness. Eddie became an enemy. In other words I did not like him. I rejected him and because of him the devil robbed my peace. Then one day during my prayer time, I read,

> *"But I say unto you, Love your enemies, bless them that curse you, do good to them that hate you, and pray for them which despitefully use you, and persecute you."* (Matthew 5:44)

I obeyed the word of God and began to prayer for Eddie, who in my opinion persecuted my pastor. Two or three years later, I left my beloved Baptist Church to attend the Seminary. The person I loved the most in my departure was Eddie. Praying for him turned my bitterness into forgiveness and love. In your marriage relationship, prayer daily for your spouse. Refuse to let the sun go down on any hurt or unforgiveness. At night, men pray with your wife and for your wife, and the peace of God will keep your marriage in one accord, strong and healthy.

Five motivations for forgiveness that will maintain a strong and joyous marriage:

1. **Always remember that forgiveness is the centerpiece of your freedom**. Freedom to love, to live and to laugh.

Forgiveness is vertical: *"If we say that we have no sin, we deceive ourselves, and the truth is not in us"* (John 1:8). But, *"If we confess our sins, he is faithful and just to forgive us our sins, and to cleanse us from all unrighteousness"* (I John 1:9). Over the forty-eight years of serving Him, I have mastered a freedom in Christ through the blood of Jesus. I have discovered that there is no sin greater than the blood. And that we serve the Father of mercies. He is ready to forgive, to deliver, and to restore.

In forgiveness, I experience horizontal freedom. Through forgiveness, I have peace with all men. Through forgiveness my wife and I are at peace. No walls, no silent treatments but a loving relationship through forgiveness. The atmosphere of my home is one of peace. It is my refuge, my haven, my place of rest! Yes, forgiveness is the key to your joy and freedom. It releases the ability to love yourself and to love others. I am not stupid but I do at least seven stupid things a week. I have to forgive myself for stupid actions, words or mistakes. If forgiveness doesn't happen, you won't happen. You will not flow in the joy and peace of the Holy Spirit. If forgiveness doesn't happen your marriage won't happen. It will not be a place of bliss and joy. So daily, live in a spirit of forgiveness. Be slow to speak, quick to forgive, and quick to let it go!

2. The second motivation for forgiveness in order to have a strong marriage and close relationships is this scripture:

> ***"And forgive us our debts, as we forgive our debtors."*** (Matthew 6:12)

The truth is, when you refuse to forgive your husband or wife, a relative or a friend you are asking God not to forgive you! The acid test of your relationship to God is to forgive others!

> *"For if ye forgive men their trespasses, your heavenly Father will also forgive you: [15] But if ye forgive not men their trespasses, neither will your Father forgive your trespasses."* (Matthew 6:14-15)

3. The third motivation for forgiveness: **It is the divine link to a heart of faith**. The Holy Spirit and the Life of Faith cannot flow through a heart of unforgiveness. Marcus Aurelius was a Roman Emperor who feared God. He said to himself every morning, "Today you will meet unpleasant people who may hurt you, injure you and insult you. But you cannot live in hurt or insult, you know better. For you are a man in whom the Spirit of God dwells." I heard someone say, "Only forgiven people are going to heaven." I say, "Only forgiven people who are forgiving are going to heaven!"

Two keys to a believer who moves in the faith of God to remove mountains of difficulties: First, a heart not a head decree,

> *"If you will say to your mountain, be removed and not* ***doubt in your heart****, but believe from your heart that those things which you say shall happen, you will have whatsoever you say..."* (Mark 11:23)

Secondly, live in an attitude of forgiveness is *"...when ye stand praying, forgive, if ye have ought against any: that your Father also which is in heaven may forgive you your trespasses"* (Mark 11:25). Note: Unforgiveness is by far the main cause of a dead battery of faith. No life of forgiveness, no spirit of faith and victory. Today, choose forgiveness: Just let it go!

4. The fourth motivation for forgiveness in maintaining a strong marriage and close relationships: **Forgive to escape the tormentors**! Jesus taught unlimited forgiveness.

> *"Then came Peter to him, and said, Lord, how oft shall my brother sin against me, and I forgive him? till seven times? [22] Jesus saith unto him, I say not unto thee, Until seven times: but, Until seventy times seven."* (Matthew 18:21-22)

For every offense and every disagreement or disappointment in our marriage we are commanded to forgive 70 X 7.

Jesus gave us an example of unlimited forgiveness. In Matthew 18:23-22, He said a compassionate King forgave one of his subjects 10,000 talents which is the equivalent to $150,000 in U.S. currency. This is a picture of the cross: Christ died for us while we were yet sinners. We were redeemed by the precious blood of the Lamb. He paid a price He did not owe. He paid a price we could not pay. Then in the parable of unlimited forgiveness, Matthew 18:28-30, the forgiven was himself not forgiving. The servant whom $150,000.00 was forgiven would not forgive a man who owed 100 pence which is $28.00 in U.S. currency. The king cast the unforgiving servant into prison and delivered him to the tormentors, *v*.32-

34. Then, our Heavenly Father warned that you and I would be turned over to the tormentors if we do not forgive everyone, which includes our spouses their trespasses, *v*.35.

I was on a mission trip in Bangkok, Thailand in 1980. I was rooming with a fellow pastor and we had a disagreement. In the midst of the silly disagreement, I raised my voice in anger towards him. I went to bed with the unresolved anger and the Lord turned me over to the tormentors. It was a deep demonic torment that brought fear, confusion, and anxiety into my mind. I began to cry out to God for relief, then He spoke, "Do not you ever raise your voice in anger to one of my servants again!" I immediately repented. And instantly the Holy Spirit delivered me and peace flooded my mind. That was thirty-six years ago. I have never raised my voice in anger again or went to bed with offended, unresolved heated anger!

5. The fifth motivation for forgiveness: **Avoiding the danger of eternal judgments.**

> *"Follow peace with all men, and holiness, without which no man shall see the Lord."* (Hebrews 12:14)

Follow peace: Be in right relationship with all men. Let there be no walls of anger or resentment between you or anyone. Let that begin in your home. Then the fear of the Lord will deliver us from all unforgiveness:

"Looking diligently lest any man fail of the grace of God; lest any root of bitterness springing up trouble you, and thereby many be defiled." (Hebrews 12:15)

Refuse to stay offended. Refuse to live in anger or bitterness. Choose God's way, forgive 70 X 7. And the peace of God which surpasses all understanding or human reasoning will keep your hearts and minds in Christ Jesus. Remember, no one's wrong words or actions is worth your peace and joy in the Holy Ghost. Forgive! Just let it go in Jesus name!

Chapter Five

The Pillar of Honor for a Secure and Strong Marriage

Up front, believe this, a life, a home, a marriage not built on the Word of God will not stand. Matthew 7:24-27 states that when the storms of life come whoever builds his house on God's word will stand because it is founded on the rock. Then those who don't, when the storms of life come it falls because it was built on sand (paraphrased). Therefore to have a strong marriage that stands in the storms of life, you must build on the Word of God and on the pillar of honor.

God is the fountain head of honor. Honor flows from the kingdom of heaven not the kingdom of darkness.

> *He shall call upon me, and I will answer him: I will be with him in trouble; I will deliver him, and* ***honour him****."* (Psalms 91:15)

Honor means to show great respect or to hold in high

regard; it means to value; to hold someone in high esteem in your heart. Honor in the marriage or any close relationship begins in the heart before it has expression in words and actions. God said, "…with their lips they do honor me, but have removed their heart far from me…" In my marriage, I have a heart-felt honor for Marvelous Mary. And where there is honor in the marriage, in the home or in the church, there is an outbreak of the favor of the Lord. In other words, as I honor my wife, God's favor is upon me. I am blessed going in and blessed going out!

Honor is all over the Bible:

1. Honor the Lord: *"**Honour the LORD** with thy substance, and with the firstfruits of all thine increase."* (Proverbs 3:9); *"By humility and the fear of the LORD are riches, **and honour**, and life."* (Proverbs 22:4)
2. The Proverbs 31 woman of excellence: Proverbs 31:25, *"**Strength and honour** are her clothing; and she shall rejoice in time to come."*
3. **Honor** thy father and thy mother. *"**Honour** thy father and thy mother: that thy days may be long upon the land which the LORD thy God giveth thee."* (Exodus 20:12)
4. **Honor** widows. *"**Honour** widows that are widows indeed."* (I Timothy 5:3)
5. Teaching elders are counted worthy of **double honor**. *"Let the elders that rule well be counted*

> *worthy of* ***double honour****, especially they who labour in the word and doctrine."* (I Timothy 5:17)

Over the years, I have gradually learned the value and the anointing of honor.

> *"Wherefore the* L*ORD God of Israel saith, I said indeed that thy house, and the house of thy father, should walk before me for ever: but now the* L*ORD saith, Be it far from me; for* ***them that honour me I will honour****, and they that despise me shall be lightly esteemed."* (I Samuel 2:30)

Recently the churches of the Network of Related Pastors honored Mary and I. They purchased us an Alaskan Cruise. They also gave $20,000 to start Lynne's House. Lynne's House is in memory of my oldest daughter who tragically lost her life to deep depression. Our goal is to open it in the winter of 2016 or early spring of 2017. We will take in mentally oppressed women to set the captives free. Those pastors who honored us, God's favor and blessings will be poured out on their personal lives and local church bodies.

In other words, God rewards those who honor others. I am reminded how Elisha served and honored Elijah. As God took Elijah up by a whirlwind into heaven, a double mantle of Elijah's anointing fell on Elisha. Honor activated God's favor and blessing on Elisha (II Kings 2:1-13).

I am writing on this pillar to encourage honor in your

marriage. The scripture gives us instructions on how to do it in regards to the husband and the wife. Ladies, listed are five expressions of honor to your husband:

1. **Honor him as your head**.

"For the husband is the head of the wife, even as Christ is the head of the church: and he is the saviour of the body." (Ephesians 5:23)

I am the head of Marvelous Mary. I do not rule over her like a macho man. As her head, I serve her. As the head of my marriage and home, I protect her and provide for her. As her head, I keep our finances in order and when we had children in our home I was the chief disciplinarian. The buck always stopped with me and she was free of stress and worry and anxiety. Therefore, it was easy for her to honor me as our head.

2. **Honor him by being a good helpmeet**.

"And the LORD God said, It is not good that the man should be alone; I will make him an help meet for him." (Genesis 2:18)

Marvelous Mary is my helpmeet, she completes me. She helps me to make right decisions for our home by giving sound and godly advice. Sometimes but seldom she goes too far by trying to correct me. I lovingly tell her that she is not my mama, don't correct me! I work in piles. I have by my bed a pile of books. By my prayer couch, I have a pile of bibles and papers where I build messages or write books. She complains and tries to correct me. I tell her that she is not my mamma. As I share this I know most of you ladies are thinking this is not a correction, this is just the direction of a normal housewife. You are probably right but I am having fun justifying my messy ways.

3. **Honor him with submission.**

"Wives, submit yourselves unto your own husbands, as unto the Lord." (Ephesians 5:22)

During our marriage seminars, I jokingly share that Marvelous Mary and I have been married fifty plus years. We have been happily married for thirty years. For twenty years the word submit was too hard of a word for a feisty Cajun lady. She found a weaker translation that said, "Adapt to your husband." She declared I can do that, "adapt to Rod!" This happened thirty years ago, so for thirty years, we have been happily married. Good report: She adapts ninety-five percent of the time. After all, she is still a human being!

4. **Honor your husband with reverence.**

"However, each man among you [without exception] is to love his wife as his very own self [with behavior worthy of respect and esteem,

always seeking the best for her with an attitude of lovingkindness], and the wife [must see to it] that she respects and delights in her husband [that she notices him and prefers him and treats him with loving concern, treasuring him, honoring him, and holding him dear]." (Ephesians 5:33 AMP)

I pointed out to Mary one day that it says to hold me in awe. She replied, in her feisty mannerism, "Awe Rod!" Ladies, when you stand angrily toe to toe with your husband he shuts you down. He turns you off. His male ego is offended. Your husband's greatest need is not sex. It is your reverence and respect. You are called and commanded and anointed to honor him all the days of your life. You are not anointed to cuss and fuss at him even when he might deserve it. E.V. Hill was an anointed pastor, great preacher, and a moral statesman. Over a tape, I heard him preach at his wife's funeral, her pet name was "Baby." He tells of her love and honor towards him. He came home from work one evening, the house was dark with a candlelight on the table and the smell of delicious food cooking on their gas stove. He went to the restroom to wash his hands and when he clicked on the light switch there was no light. He rushed back to the kitchen and asked Baby what was wrong with the electricity. She replied, "You forgot to pay the electric bill, so I made the best of it by cooking you a candle light dinner." She had every right to fuss and correct, but rather gave him reverence and honor. What a lady! What a great marriage! All because of honor. By the way, he never forgot to pay a bill again.

5. Finally Ladies, **honor him by supporting him in all his ways, his life and his decisions**; even when he fails.

> *"Her husband is known in the* [city's] *gates, When he sits among the elders of the land."* (Proverbs 31:23)

Marvelous Mary is my best cheerleader. She tells me that I am her favorite preacher. Every morning when she awakes, she tells me, "I love you!" When I come home from work, she is dressed up and made up and greets me with a smile. Hot dog! In my younger years of ministry, from age 30 to 33, I was a Baptist minister. I was a zealous revival preacher. Churches in Louisiana and Mississippi would have me do week-end revivals. On one occasion, Brother Strother, an old Baptist warhorse in Oakdale, Louisiana had me in for the weekend. While there, he gave me godly counsel, in regards to my wife. "No one loves you and knows you like your wife. Listen to her. She is your best critic!" Truer words were never said. One example of this is when I pastored Reserve Church, a growing work in Reserve, Louisiana. In my zeal I loudly declared from the pulpit, "Get in or get out. This is the church of God's marines!" Later that day at home Mary asked me, "Are the people of our church, your subjects or God's subjects?" I said, "Of course, they are God's subjects." Then she replied, "What right do you have to tell them to get in or get out?" Case closed! Your wife is your best critic.

Let's move on to the best part of honor in the marriage. **Husbands, honor your wife!**

> *"In the same way, you husbands, live with your wives in an understanding way [with great gentleness and tact, and with an intelligent regard for the marriage relationship], as with [a] someone physically weaker, since she is a woman.* ***Show her honor and respect*** *as a fellow heir of the grace of life, so that your prayers will not be hindered or ineffective."* (I Peter 3:7)

Listed are several expressions of honor to your wife:

1. **Don't attack her weaknesses**. I have learned the more I have tried to fix my wife by pointing out her weaknesses, the more I fail her. The end result, I dishonor her!

Men, if we major on the minors, the weakness or the flaws of our wife, you minister rejection and death. The more I have majored on Mary's weaknesses, the more I have entrapped her in her weakness. Husbands, honor her by majoring on her strengths, not her weaknesses. She knows about her weaknesses. She knows about her human flaws and is doing her best to daily overcome them.

2. **Honor her by not correcting her in front of the children or anyone else.** This is very degrading and disrespectful.

"The spirit of a man will sustain his infirmity; but a wounded spirit who can bear?" (Proverbs 18:14)

To correct her publically is to dishonor her and wound her spirit. Men be slow to anger and be slow to speak. In regards to publically correcting anyone, hold your peace. A fool is compulsive and full of words.

3. Along the same thought lines **honor her by not attacking her with anger**. Anger does not work the righteousness of God. A proud man tries to control his wife and children with anger. This is a carnal method of control and it is a form of witchcraft. It will divide and destroy a marriage.

"A soft answer turneth away wrath: but ***grievous words stir up anger****. [2] The tongue of the wise useth knowledge aright: but the mouth of fools poureth out foolishness."* (Proverbs 15:1-2)

Over forty-five years ago, I was invited to preach on a Sunday in a small river town of Donaldsonville, Louisiana. We traveled in on the Saturday evening and on the way I got angry with the wife of my youth and yelled at her. That night, I went to the church building to pray because my spirit man was grieved about the blow-out. As I knelt the Holy Spirit corrected me, "Don't ever raise your voice against your wife again!" I repented. It has been forty-five years. Never again!

4. **Honor her with a listening ear**.

> *"Wherefore, my beloved brethren, let every man be swift to hear, slow to speak, slow to wrath."* (James 1:19)

The second chapter of this book is about the Pillar of Listening for a Happy Marriage. So I will not expound on it again. But a listening ear declares – I have time for you; I will learn of you; I love you! A listener is a true lover of your soul.

5. **Honor her by being the chief disciplinarian of your home**. A godly leader in the home should be this:

> *"One that ruleth well his own house, having his children in subjection with all gravity."* (I Timothy 3:4)

A father/husband who is godly and desires to honor his wife will manage the children and keep them obedient under the authority of the home which includes the mother. I am sharing a personal example of a husband taking his place and authority as the chief disciplinarian of the home. One evening, returning from work, I encountered a very frustrated mother. Our last three children of the five were staircased, each about eighteen months apart. In their misbehavior, they had pushed Marvelous Mary to her limits. As I gathered the three around me I firmly stated, "That's my wife you are messing with!" Their eyes filled with fear knowing they had crossed a boundary. Then, I simply obeyed God's word and spanked them with the rod of correction. As I prayed with them into repentance, peace filled my home. God was honored! My wife was honored! And the three children got right with God and their parents!

6. **Honor her by giving her a compliment a day.**

> *"Death and life are in the power of the tongue: and they that love it shall eat the fruit thereof.* [22] *Whoso findeth a wife findeth a good thing, and obtaineth favour of the LORD."* (Proverbs 18:21-22)

I explained and expounded on the Pillar of Communication in chapter one. One additional comment in over our fifty-seven years, my wife and I have learned not to talk down to each other. During the day, I find ways to compliment her: "You are beautiful." "You are my woman." "I don't deserve you." "You are so good to me!" It is true, your wife will become what you feed her with your words. A compliment a day will keep the devil away and it will put honey into her tank. Again, "If you want honey, speak honey!"

7. **Finally, honor her by not only praying for her but by praying with her on a consistent basis.**

> *"...the head of the woman is man..."* (Ephesians 5:23)

As her head, she desperately needs you as her spiritual covering to protect her from the fiery darts of the devil and protect her from the emotional pressure in the storms of life. My oldest daughter was bipolar. Eight years ago at the age of forty-four she committed suicide in my bedroom after finding my 38 caliber pistol. That night as we laid in bed twisting and weeping, Mary said, "Rod my heart is about to burst!" As her head and covering I cried out to the Lord, "Help!" And He did! During the week and ensuing months grace and peace filled our hearts and mind. Husbands, you need to carry out one of your most important responsibilities. Cover your wife. Be her hero! Be her spiritual leader. Honor her by praying daily for her and nightly with her.

CHAPTER SIX

The Pillar of Loyalty

As I begin to write this chapter on loyalty, I thought to tie-in the thought of faithfulness, giving the full picture of a loyal spouse. See it as you read these scriptures on the faithful.

> *"A talebearer revealeth secrets: but he that is of a **faithful spirit** concealeth the matter."* (Proverbs 11:13)

> *"A wicked messenger falleth into mischief: but a **faithful ambassador** is health."* (Proverbs 13:17)

> *"A **faithful witness** will not lie: but a false witness will utter lies."* (Proverbs 14:5)

> *"Most men will proclaim everyone his own goodness: but a **faithful man** who can find?"* (Proverbs 20:6)

I want to focus on what Proverbs 20:6 stated, *"...a **faithful man** who can find?"* A true statement in a nation where one out of two marriages are in the divorce courts. A faithful person is one who shows a true constant support of loyalty. Another Webster's definition of faithful is not having sex with someone who is not your wife or husband. Synonyms for faithful are steadfast, steady, true blue, **loyal**! Antonyms for faithful are faithless, unfaithful, false, and **disloyal**!

Loyalty in its root meaning is someone who lives by principles and moral obligations rather than by feelings or situations. Loyalty actually means you are faithful; you are committed to your marriage, to the cause of Christ, without reservations or certain conditions. My wife, Marvelous Mary is loyal to God, loyal to me as her husband, loyal to her children and grandchildren, and loyal to the body without any reservation. Loyalty is royalty. The husband and wife's loyalty to each other should be a reflection of Ruth's relationship to Naomi;

> *"And she said, Behold, thy sister in law is gone back unto her people, and unto her gods: return thou after thy sister in law.*
> *16 And Ruth said, Intreat me not to leave thee, or to return from following after thee: for whither thou goest, I will go; and where thou lodgest, I will lodge: thy people shall be my people, and thy God my God:*
> *17 Where thou diest, will I die, and there will I be buried: the*

Lord do so to me, and more also, if ought but death part thee and me." (Ruth 1:15-17)

I must boast on the loyalty of my wife. Her loyalty to me is until death parts. In 1968, I was born again and called into the ministry in early 1969. I was a supervisor at Air Products and Chemical. In my calling, I made a decision to go to the New Orleans Baptist Seminary in New Orleans. In this decision we had to uproot from our home, our local church, our close friends and a career with financial security. She left her security to follow me, to lodge where I lodged, to be with me in spite of her fears for our future. Loyalty is royalty!

Marriage is a covenant, a divine union of a man and a woman. There is no real covenant unless first there is a heart-felt loyalty. Let's see loyalty in the content of Malachi 2:13-14.

> *"And this have ye done again, covering the altar of the Lord with tears, with weeping, and with crying out, insomuch that he regardeth not the offering any more, or receiveth it with good will at your hand. [14] Yet ye say, Wherefore? Because the Lord hath been witness between thee and the wife of thy youth,* ***against whom thou hast dealt treacherously****: yet is she thy companion, and the wife of thy covenant."*

The husband dealt treacherously with the wife of his

youth. He broke faith with her. He was unfaithful or disloyal. Too often, I have been in counsel with couples where one of the spouses has been disloyal by violating the marriage covenant through adultery. So heartbreaking to the violated husband or wife. Shocking and heart shattering to say the least.

In the world's system marriage is a contract. A contract is not a covenant. A contract can be broken with little or no consequences. A contract is based on various obligations being met. For example in a marriage where there is not a covenant commitment this attitude is common, "If you do this I am happy. If not, I am out of here!" A contract is void of heart-felt loyalty.

In God's Kingdom, marriage is not a contract, it is a covenant. It is a merger where a man and woman are loyal to each other, until death parts.

> *"And Adam said, **This is now bone of my bones, and flesh of my flesh**: she shall be called Woman, because she was taken out of Man. [24] Therefore shall a man leave his father and his mother, and shall cleave unto his wife: and they shall be one flesh."* (Genesis 2:23-24)

This passage contains the loyalty language of a marriage: you are bone of my bone and flesh of my flesh. In the marriage covenant, we are one and inseparable. A man shall leave his parents and cleave to his wife. Leave and cleave is covenant language. Cleave means to adhere firmly, to have unwavering loyalty; to stick; super natural glue. They shall be one flesh; integrated in spirit, mind and body. A sacred union that is not to be violated by strange flesh.

> *"The wife is bound by the law as long as her husband liveth; but if her husband be dead, she is at liberty to be married to whom she will; only in the Lord."* (I Corinthians 7:39)

The marriage law is an inseparable covenant relationship written by the Spirit on the born-again believer's heart. It is not flour glue or contract love. It is the supernatural glue of Holy Ghost covenant love. Loyalty is royalty.

Loyalty stands with you on your worst day. Loyalty supports you even in your mistakes and failures. In 2007, I borrowed over $400,000 to build a new cabin in the foothills of Pigeon Forge. Cabins were selling quickly so you could build and sell one with a forty thousand profit. I went against my debt free teachings and my wife's warning, "Do not do it!" In 2008 the cabin was completed and ready for sale. In the same time period, the real estate bubble popped and by the time I sold it, I lost $80,000. Mary was Mrs. Loyalty, she never said I told you so. She never hammered me over a very unwise investment. Rather in her loyalty, she stood by her man! Grateful!

Loyalty refuses to entertain unfound criticism. Several years ago, a couple we respected took us out for dinner. Little did we know that this was a farewell meeting to us as their pastors. During this farewell dinner, he proceeded to tell me about my flaws and faults. In the midst of it, my loyal wife interrupted him, "I live with this man. He is true-blue. He loves God and loves people. You have no grounds for your accusations." Loyalty is royalty! It is a pillar of a solid marriage.

Loyalty is covenant expression. It will cover the back of someone's short-comings whether it be a spouse, a relative or a friend. Genesis 9:21-24 declares the story of three young sons. Their father Noah was drunk and laid naked in his tent. Ham went and looked upon his father's nakedness and proceeded to tell his two brothers. The other two sons went into theirs father's tent backwards and covered their father's nakedness. In their covenant loyalty they covered their Papa's state of dishonor. Loyalty is royalty.

To be loyal means that it will redefine other relationships. My marriage redefined my relationship with other women. In my loyalty to my wife, I am not looking. In my young life, I was a womanizer. Loyalty to my covenant marriage has redefined my lifestyle.

Marriage life, church, friendship, and relationships must be built upon loyalty because there is going to be conflict. It is a rule of life that in any close relationships there will be disagreements and disappointments. There will be a temptation to disconnect. I heard it taught that there are two basic types of personalities in a marriage conflict: skunks and turtles.

1. **The Skunk**: If the skunk type spouse doesn't like what is going on or feels pressure, he or she will stink up the whole place with an emotional outburst. Most women are skunks who have not learned how to handle marriage conflicts. They are reactors rather than responders. A few years ago, my wife and I decided to put stucco on the outside walls but leave half the vinyl siding up to give it a wainscot look. The contractor misunderstood and ripped all my vinyl off on one side. I was out of town, so Mary made the decision to go with the full stucco look. When I returned I firmly disagreed and told her to stop the job and have them put half of the vinyl siding back in place. She skunked-out on me. She began to weep and said to me, "Just bring me to a mental ward, this will cause me to have a nervous breakdown!" In my loyalty to her heart, the skunk won the day.

2. **The Turtle**: When conflict happens, the turtle spouse just shrinks back into his shell, becomes quiet and distant. This is the typical male response. I use to call it breaking fellowship. In my disagreement, I would simply give Mary the quiet treatment. My wife would confront this negative turtle behavior and I would reply, "God breaks fellowship when we sin!" Maybe so, but Rod is not God. Hormonally, skunks tend to marry turtles and usually a mutual ground of compromise and understanding is worked out. If two skunks marry, it is a nightmare of spewing and stinking. Only loyalty and faithfulness to the covenant will keep these two together. So be it in my fifty-seven years of marriage, the skunk and the turtle declare that loyalty is royalty!

So as a couple, you must build on the pillar of loyalty. Six common sense principles of loyalty to avoid or manage conflict in your marriage:

1. **Don't compare!** Too often in my early years of marriage, the merging years, I would compare my wife to another wife as an example to improve her behavior. Wrong move! We are not to compare flesh with flesh or personality with personality. Men, rejoice in the wife of your youth. Ladies look to your husband as your hero, not another!

2. **Be loyal, don't condemn**. Don't hammer on the flaws or faults of your spouse. Don't make comments, "You are just like your dad, full of anger." "You are just like your mother, controlling."

3. **Don't challenge every statement**: "You are not saying it right!"

4. **Don't condescend or treat your husband or wife life a small child**. Be loyal, respect your husband or wife's adulthood. I jokingly share with Mary when she tries to correct me, "Mary, you are not my mamma, don't try to correct me!" In reality, she is really trying to complete me because she loves me and wants me to be the best in my ministry, my fatherhood and my role as her spouse.

5. **Husbands be loyal to your role as the head of**

your home: serve and lead but don't command your wife. God has not anointed us as macho men to demand hot meals, hot coffee and hot lips.

6. **As husband and wife, obey the Word of God.** Refuse to complain. Rather, in all things give thanks. Let's be loyal to the Holy Spirit and create an atmosphere of praise in our home that He can inhabit! Loyalty is royalty!

Chapter Seven

The Pillar of Communion: A Consistent Devotional Life

In my first chapter, The Pillar of Communication, I referred to Dr. James Dobson's three-fold prescription for a great marriage. One of the three truths for a successful marriage was a common devotion life. Remember, we are a spirit who lives in a body who has a mind. Our spirit man is made up of three parts:

1. **Conscience**: The seat of knowing right from wrong. The area where the Holy Spirit brings conviction of sin and also His direction for righteousness.

2. **Intuition**: The place were faith is borne, to know something without any proof or evidence. The place where we know the gifts of the Holy Spirit and move in them to meet the needs and sufferings of others.

3. **Communion**: Where the spirit man comprehends who God is and worships Him as Lord and Savior. In our heart of hearts where we love God and enjoy His presence, God is

with us and God is in us! In that overflow of His presence, we love others. Therefore, as our spirit man matures; as we are transformed and conformed into His image, our love for others becomes unconditional and giving. In our marriage, as we develop our devotional life, a deepening of love and appreciation of each other has no limits.

Allow me to give you direction or vision for sustaining a growing relationship with the Lord and with each other. By morning, develop the discipline of sitting and communing at the feet of Jesus. Mary, a devoted follower of Lord Jesus Christ set the example.

> *"And Martha had a sister called Mary, **which sat at the feet and heard His word**."* (Luke 10:39)

Just about every morning at daybeak, it has been my habit for over thirty years, to sit at the feet of Jesus and hear His word. This is the key to go from faith to faith and from glory to glory. The Psalmist declared,

> *"O God, thou art my God; **early will I seek** thee… my soul thirsteth for the…"* (Psalms 63:1)

In my notes, I have written down these two quotes. I don't know who to give credit to: "Holy is the day when dawn finds me on the mountain top with God. Blessed is the day when morning is sanctified…set apart to God."

Every morning, at the feet of Jesus I experience what I

call "Divine Osmosis." I sit still and absorb the grace of God: grace to see the will of God, grace to be the will of God, and grace to do the will of God! Again, the psalmist declared,

> *"Let all that I am **wait quietly before God**..."* (Psalms 62:5 NLT)

As you quietly wait on God in the morning, you have grace to declare that He is my rock; He is my salvation; He is my defense: I shall not be moved. He is my glory. Yes, He is the rock of my strength. Strength to love my wife as I ought to love her. Furthermore, as I wait, I see Him as my refuge; my safe haven, my place of protection and peace (Psalms 62:6-7 paraphrased)! I bring this place of protection and peace into my marriage and my home.

As you wait, it is the place to see your dreams and your divine destiny. In the book of Habakkuk, the prophet was in the midst of a nation in crisis. His nation was full of evil and injustice and they were facing impending judgment. The prophet's response to the crisis was,

> *"...I will wait to see...I will stand upon my tower and watch to see what He will say to me."* (Habakkuk 2:2)

The Lord responded and gave him a word to write the vision upon a tablet, a direction to live by. God's further instruction was to keep waiting for the vision for it had an appointed time (Habakkuk 2:3). In the morning as I wait, I receive direction and marching orders for the day. I renew a sense of purpose in serving God and others. Some things I am seeing—like a Third Great Awakening—has not happened. But I am waiting and expecting!

Several years ago, I crashed an outing my two daughters gave my wife for Mother's Day. They reserved a hotel room in the New Orleans area and took her for lunch the next day at an exclusive restaurant on Magazine Street. I went along to celebrate this special occasion. Later that afternoon, one of my daughters challenged me, "Daddy, why do you bark at mother the way you do?" That statement brought conviction upon my heart that I was not honoring my wife. The next morning I wrote out a confession of faith and commitment at the feet of Jesus, "I receive a Baptism of Grace to adore and cherish my wife!" So daily, I receive the grace of God to love, to cherish and adore my wife. Men, build a strong marriage by daily sitting at the feet of Jesus!

Our Lord's response to a busy and anxious Martha who was complaining about Mary's lack of serving was this,

> *"Martha, ...one thing is needful and Mary has chosen that good portion which shall never be taken away from her."* (Luke 10:42)

He said, "One thing is needful! Mary sat at the feet of Jesus and heard his word." Again, all that I am is borne at daybreak at the feet of Jesus. My grace to love and serve others is borne at the feet of Jesus. My grace to move in the faith and purposes of God is borne at the feet of Jesus. My grace to adore and cherish my wife is borne at the feet of Jesus.

Isaiah the prophet declared this truth,

> *"They that* ***wait upon the Lord*** *shall renew their strength; they shall mount up wings as an eagles; they shall run and not be weary; and they shall walk and not faint."* (Isaiah 40:31)

So by morning, wait upon the Lord! As you do, He will renew your strength. Renew means there is an exchange of strength; your human strength for His strength. As you wait, the Holy Spirit will refresh you with the upper springs and the lower springs. The prophet Hosea declared the word of the Lord,

> *"I will be like the dew to Israel..."* (Hosea 14:5)

Dew is the source of refreshment and replenishment to the earth. The dew of early morning refreshes the grass, the flowers and the crops of the laboring farmers. I read somewhere that dew will not fall in the heat of the day or when the wind is blowing. Rather, the air must be still and in the stillness of the night invisible particles of moisture form to replenish the plants. "Be still and know that I am God..." (Psalms 46:10). To be still and know Him is to love Him. And the more you know Him and love Him, the more you love others. Again, as I wrote in chapter one, the more I relate to the Lord vertically, the better I relate to my wife and others horizontally.

When Mary sat at Jesus' feet, **she heard His word**! Hearing is one of the most important words in the Bible. The revelator made this statement to the seven churches.

> *"He that hath an ear,* ***let him hear*** *what the* ***spirit saith*** *unto the churches; to him that overcometh will I give to eat of the tree of life..."* (Revelations 2:7)

The Holy Spirit made it quite clear that faith comes by hearing the word of God, that is by the rhema word or the quickened word. The verse must become the voice. The said word must become the saying word. There is a place in God where we are hearing with our third ear...our spirit man. Let's follow the example of our Lord Jesus in being still and hearing the voice of His heavenly Father.

> *"Very early in the morning, having arisen a long while before daybreak. He went out and departed to a solitary place to pray."* (Mark 1:35)

He went to a quiet place at daybreak. This proceeded a season of preaching in the synagogues, healing the sick and casting out demons. My advice for an overcoming life and a happy marriage: **early in the morning have a quiet time in a**

certain place! The same anointing that empowered our Lord will empower you!

By morning at the feet of Jesus, build your life and your marriage on the pillar of communion. **At the feet of Jesus we develop a spirit of repentance and dependence**. In Luke 5:4-8, Peter had an encounter with the Lord. At our Lord's word he let down his net and enclosed a great multitude of fish that broke his net. He called his partners and they filled their boats with so many fish that their boats began to sink. Because of his greed, he fell down at Jesus feet and said to Jesus, *"Depart from me, for I am a sinful man, O Lord"* (Luke 5:8). I am not sin conscious or guilt ridden, but I still have a human nature. I still have carry-over from the old man: pockets of selfishness, pride and lust. I still sin, and there are moments in my life that I fall short of the glory of God. So by morning, I enforce the victory of Calvary:

1. **I take the blood for my sin**.

> *"If we say that we have no sin, we deceive ourselves, and the truth is not in us. [9] If we confess our sins, he is faithful and just to forgive us our sins, and to cleanse us from all unrighteousness."*
> (I John 1:8-9)

I am so grateful that there is no sin greater than the blood of Jesus. I am a blood breather: I breathe the blood in and I breathe sin out! Join me!

2. **I take the cross for my selfishness.**

> *"Knowing this, that our old man is crucified with him, that the body of sin might be destroyed, that henceforth we should not serve sin."* (Romans 6:6)

> *"Likewise reckon ye also yourselves to be dead unto sin..."* (Romans 6:11)

So by morning, I reckon my old man co-crucified with Christ...the lust of my eye, the lust of my flesh and the pride of life. The two roots of all sin in the believers life are lust and pride.

3. By morning, ***"I reckon myself alive unto God through Jesus Christ my Lord!"*** (Romans 6:11).

I reckon myself **co-resurrected** with Christ Jesus. Alive unto His presence, His purity, His power and His purposes. By doing so, His life and love flow freely through me to touch others. Also, His life and love will flow through me to cherish my wife. Join me!

4. **By morning, I enforce the victory of Calvary in declaring myself co-healed** with Christ Jesus.

> *"...surely He bore our sicknesses and our pains."* (Isaiah 53:4)

> *"...And with His scourging we are healed."* (Isaiah 53:5)

He was made sick with our sicknesses that we might be made whole and healthy with His health and healing. I reckon it so. Join me! I want to stay healthy. I want to serve my wife, my children and the body of Christ with full strength.

By morning at the feet of Jesus, **we live out the great commandment to love God with all our heart, soul, and mind.** We see a beautiful picture of this when the woman of sin falls at the feet of Jesus with an alabaster box of anointment.

> *"...**she stood at His feet** behind Him weeping and she began to **wash His feet** with tears (apparently down at His feet) she did **wipe his feet** with the hairs of her head, and **she kissed His feet** and **anointed His feet** with the ointment."* (Luke 7:38)

This is a prophetic progression of a true follower of our Lord Jesus. First and foremost, **we become a waiter**; we sit at the feet of Jesus. A waiter always **becomes a worshipper**; we kiss the feet of Jesus. We love Him with all our heart, soul and mind. Then a worshipper **becomes a warrior**. As we wait and worship, the grace of God empowers us to war against the darkness and demons. We keep our home and marriage free, then we set captives free. Finally, **a warrior becomes a witness**. By the anointing, we heal the broken hearted, we preach the gospel to the poor, we set the captives free, and we liberate those who have bruised hearts. Join me in the morning at the feet of Jesus!

By morning, at the feet of Jesus **we war for our home, our marriage, our church, and our nation.** The Bible tells of a man by the name of Jarius who warred for his home. He had a twelve year old daughter that lay dying.

> *"...he fell down at* ***Jesus feet*** *and besought him that he would come into his house."* (Luke 8:42)

Then later on his way to the Dad's house, the daughter died and a report came for Jesus not to come. Jesus said,

> *"Fear not, believe only and she shall be made whole"* (Luke 8:50)

Our Lord raised her from the dead. Jarius had fallen at **His feet** warring or appealing on behalf of his daughter. The devil's main target is your home: your marriage and your children. Marvelous Mary and I do nightly warfare for our children and grandchildren. We take the Lamb of God and the blood covering and protecting their homes. We release healing into sick bodies of people we know and love. We serve Jehovah Nissa, our Man of War. We live in a war zone and we honor His promises. We declare that no weapon formed against us shall prosper and every tongue that accuses us is being refuted. Over the years, early in the morning, I break every vex and hex and curse that the enemy has spoken against our household. Let's be grateful that the Lord has given us all authority over the powers of darkness and they can by no means can hurt us. Together, as a couple, we have authority to war and to win.

Finally by morning, **at the feet of Jesus we receive strength for the storms of life.** In the scripture, the Word of God tells of a woman who had an issue of blood for twelve years. She had spent all her resources on physicians, yet no healing. People isolated themselves from her because she was unclean in her bleeding. Desperate and in despair she pressed through the crowds, came behind Jesus, **went down to His feet,** and touched the hem of His garment and was made whole (Luke 8:43-46). She fell at the feet of Jesus and received the grace of healing.

> *"...somebody touched me, for I perceive that virtue is gone out of me."* (Luke 8:46)

At the feet of Jesus, we receive His grace and His strength to go through the storms, the setbacks, and the heartbreaks of life. At the age of twenty-two my oldest daughter, Lynne Aguillard Venus went into a bipolar nervous breakdown and for twenty-two years we fought for her mental health and life. At the age of forty-four, in the midst of deep depression she tragically ended her physical life. We wept a river. We refused to charge God. We received the grace of God to worship Him in the midst of our broken hearts. Then by grace, we moved forward with a greater capacity to love the hurting and the suffering. I just got off the phone with a NRP pastor in Wisconsin. I shared with him that if Mary and I didn't have a devoted communion life, we would not have survived her tragic death. If we had not been deeply connected to the body of Christ, the grief would have shattered us. Because by morning we sit at the feet of Jesus, Mary and I have strength to go through the storms of life and marriage. We have grace to deeply love each other, forgive each other, and unite as a powerful unit of prayer. Join us!

Chapter Eight

The Pillar of Integrity and Honesty

"...I will lead a life of integrity in my own home..." (Psalms 101:2)

I am beginning this chapter by defining the meaning of integrity and later apply it to a successful marriage. Integrity is adherence to moral and ethical principles. It means soundness of character and honesty. Integrity commits itself to character over personal gain or desires. It commits itself to service over power; to covenant commitment over convenience. Integrity – the root word is integer – a whole number like 1 not 1 ½. It comes from the root to complete – not ninety-nine percent but one hundred percent. As a husband and as a minister, I must be trusted on all points or I can't be trusted on any point. Integrity means an unimpaired condition like the hull of a new ship. Remembering history, the supposing integrity of the hull of the Titanic. The word out was, "Even God can't sink her!"

Sadly, one of God's icebergs sank her. Integrity belongs to a character rooted in humility. God indeed gives grace to the humble. He gives grace and strength to the lowly. He entrusts the gospel to the trustworthy and those who are teachable and faithful in all relationships!

There are several areas of personal integrity in a marriage that will make it strong and stable and successful:

1. **Financial integrity** – Being a good steward of God's money. As the husband and head of my home, the Lord holds me responsible for the oversight of the finances. First and foremost, I am honest in paying our tithes and giving offerings. Early on in our covenant relationship with the Lord, Marvelous Mary and I both saw God's commandment in bringing our tithes to the local church. We went on a budget and used cash to buy things. We cut back on all the extras: cold drinks, newspapers, eating out, etc. Over a short period of time through the nickels and dimes we found the tithe. Later, we discovered the blessings of paying our tithes. God opened the windows of Heaven and poured out financial blessing on our obedience. Within two years, we were debt free and our marriage was financially stress free. Part of having a happy marriage is bringing your tithes and offerings to the Lord's storehouse, your local church. In our marriage and financial integrity, we made a commitment to be debt free, not to use the credit system and lose our money with interest charges. I paid all our bills on time. During the forty-eight years of our walk with God, my wife hasn't known the burden and

frustration of financial pressure.

In my **Financial Integrity**, I realize the importance of honoring my wife by sharing our financial blessings. We used the ten by ten method. We tithed ten percent and saved ten percent and lived on the rest. Today, my tithe and missions giving is about thirty percent of my income, we live on the remaining seventy percent and are blessed beyond measure. She is free to shop for groceries, clothing, jewelry and giving to others without financial stress. In this we bless the Lord our Provider. We have been good stewards of finances and He has been faithful to honor our integrity.

> *"Honour the LORD with thy substance, and with the firstfruits of all thine increase: [10] So shall thy barns be filled with plenty, and thy presses shall burst out with new wine."* (Proverbs 3:9-10)

2. **Word Integrity** – When you give your word, you give your life. Your word should be dependable, faithful and honest.

> *"And the LORD said unto Satan, Hast thou considered my servant Job, that there is none like him in the earth, a perfect and an upright man, one that feareth God, and escheweth evil? And still he* ***holdeth fast his integrity****, although thou movedst me against him, to destroy him without cause."* (Job 2:3)

Marriage is a covenant – it is built upon the pillar of honesty and integrity. Marvelous Mary and I communicate daily on our whereabouts. When I leave my home in the morning, I tell her where I am going and how long I will be gone. Daily, she can track my word and activities.

I can predict Marvelous Mary. Part of integrity is to be consistent; to be predictable with your words. The scripture declares that Nathaniel was a man of no guile. He was a man of no deceit. When he gave his word, he gave his life. This describes my wife. As I write today, March 29, 2016, our fifty-seventh marriage anniversary, I can predict she will not lie. She is full of truth, a woman of no deceit. I can fully trust her word. I cannot say that about myself like I can say it about her. I have not always been fully truthful to her in regards to a major purchase. I really had to repent on one or two occasions for telling half-truths which is a lie. Several years ago, I bought a very expensive mud boat with an air cooled engine for marsh mud duck hunting. Later, Marvelous Mary asked me how much I paid for it. I mumbled a few thousand dollars. A half-truth; a breach in integrity; an open door for the devil to question her trust toward me. The mud boat and engine actually cost over twelve thousand dollars. Men, let us be trustworthy. When you buy a new shotgun, pistol or rifle don't hide it from her, rather have integrity. Be Honest, tell her the cost of your purchase and make sure she is in agreement.

The bridge of love is called trust. Love in marriage or in any other godly relationship travels over the bridge of trust.

For example, in a case of adultery the covenant of a marriage is totally violated. All trust of the innocent party is breached. In every case where I have mediated as counselor, the restoration of trust is a long process. In most cases, forgiveness is given up front to a repentative adulterer or adulteress but the repentance has to be proven and the trust has to be earned. Even when the repenting believer is sincere and the Holy Spirit does His deep work, the bridge of trust takes months to be rebuild and in some cases years. Therefore, by morning sit at the feet of Jesus and do preventative maintenance. Let the word of God go deep and keep your mind and heart renewed in the grace of God to maintain your integrity, honesty and fidelity.

> *"Thy word is a lamp unto my feet, and a light unto my path."* (Psalms 119:105)

> *"Thy word have I hid in mine heart, that I might not sin against thee."* (Psalms 119:11)

3. **Time Integrity** – A third aspect in the soundness of character and honesty. As an individual and as a couple we plan well. He who plans well has joy. Both Marvelous Mary and I plan our day, our week and even our months. Every morning I have a To-Do List that by grace I will accomplish by the end of the day. By morning, both of us sit at the feet of Jesus to get grace to face the day and to accomplish our purposes for that day. We both own an iPhone and iPad and we are on iCloud. Our calendars dictate our appointments for each day and our

ministry assignments for the month. Together, we average about three weekends a month ministering at local churches, some regional and some out of state. Each week, we minister every Thursday night in our home church. We are very busy but we accomplish much by planning well!

Also, in time integrity there is a virtue called punctuality. Punctuality is part of faithfulness. I failed once or twice with my wife in financial integrity but I am an "A" student in time integrity. Not only do I plan my day and week well, I am usually early for all my appointments and especially at church services. Marvelous Mary has not always been very punctual. With her schedule there is a lot of facial and hair preparations to meet the day. Sunday is not an exception. From the time of our marriage, 1959 until 1968, we were a one car family. Then in 1968, I got born again and began a covenant relationship with my Lord and His local body. Covenant to my local church meant that I would be on time for every church service Sunday morning, Sunday night and prayer meetings on Wednesday night. Mary was not quite as convicted as I was. After being late several times at my local church services during the first few months, I became a frustrated believer and husband. This resulted in heated discussions, better called arguments. For the peace of my home and the peace of our minds, I bit the bullet and bought a second car. For over forty-eight years, we have been a two car family because of punctuality or time integrity. Rejoicing! By the way, Marvelous Mary is now an "A-" student in punctuality. She desires to honor me and follow the leader. Men, tell your wife to read this section. It may help her to improve her punctuality.

4. **Doctrinal Integrity** – Mary and I have based our life, our home, and all of our relationships on the Word of God. We don't compromise truth or the moral absolute's of God's word. In our thinking and lifestyle, what was wrong for the first church is wrong for the last church. What was right for the first church is right for the last church. Based on our biblical convictions, it has laid a sure foundation for a happy marriage. When we had a parenting issue, we went to the Word of God. In the word, we discovered that spanking a child on his buttocks in the event of rebellion was God's will. It would deliver the child's soul from hell. We agreed and together we did it and there was peace in the valley in our home. We discovered in the Word of God that tithing was His will. Together, we tithed and gave offerings. God's word is true and we have been debt free for over thirty years. (Note there was a brief three year period I went into some debt, but never again!) A debt free home makes for a happy marriage. No financial stress or fussing.

Also, in the Word of God, we discovered that marriage is a covenant. I wrote about this in an earlier chapter. Over our fifty-seven years, we have practiced covenant. We worked through our personal conflicts and never considered separation or divorce. A covenant based marriage is a happy marriage.

5. **Relationship Integrity** – With our sons and daughters we maintained relationship integrity. We loved our

sons and daughters deeply but we never honored them above the Word of God. The Holy Spirit, early on, warned us not to commit the sin of Eli who honored his sons above the Word of God and God judged his whole household – serious stuff! When Sunday morning came around, they were all dressed sharp and in the services on time. As teenagers, they never missed a youth service. We simply honored God and kept them under the Word of God. No secular rock music was allowed in my home or cars. We limited them to one hour of television on a daily basis with a requirement to read one hour a day. No phone calls or going out with unbelievers. We had relationship integrity. We honored God's word above our sons and daughters. What we sowed, we reaped. Three are sold out to Jesus. One is in Heaven and the fifth will return to the God of His childhood.

6. **Sexual Integrity** – Every man should read the book, "Everyman's Battle" by Stephen Arterburn and Fred Stoeker. A real help for men to maintain their sexual integrity. As married men and women, all of our sexual gratification must come from our spouse. In the last chapter of this book, I have written that romance and sexual gratification in the marriage bed is a strong pillar for an enduring marriage. Sex in the marriage bed is a gift from God with a divine design of procreation and pleasure.

Please read Psalms 101:2-8 which is a biblical description of personal integrity. *"I lead a life of integrity in my own home"* (Psalms 101:2). What I am in private, I am in public. The way I treat my wife and children, my word and prayer life, what I watch and listen to and what I read is the same both in private as it is in public. Integrity says, *"I refuse to look at anything vile and vulgar"* (Psalms 101:3). I set no wicked thing before my eyes. No R-rated movies, bedroom scenes or pornography. Integrity says, I will flee from evil, *"I will reject perverse ideas and stay away from evil"* (Psalms 101:4). The fear of the Lord is to hate evil and to love righteousness. Help us Lord…grace, grace and more grace to maintain our sexual integrity.

Seven steps to moral purity in maintaining your sexual integrity (especially for men):

1. By morning, sit at the feet of Jesus and feed your heart the saying Word of God. Obey the law of sowing and reaping. *"Be not deceived; God is not mocked: for whatsoever a man soweth, that shall he also reap. [8] For he that soweth to his flesh shall of the flesh reap corruption; but he that soweth to the Spirit shall of the Spirit reap life everlasting"* (Galatians 6:7-8).
2. By morning, choose the fear of the Lord. Hate evil (sexual impurity) and love righteousness.
3. Starve the stronghold of moral impurity. Refuse to set anything wicked before your eyes.
4. Bounce your eyes. Refuse to lock in on the beauty and curves of the opposite sex. I am not a beach guy. During spring breaks, Mary and I would spend a week at Sandestin, Florida. It was our daily schedule for me

to drop Mary off at the white sands at about 11:00 AM. Later during the day, I would drive and pick her up. There were occasions that I would have to walk on the beach to escort her back to our car. On the way, the bikini clad curves would walk in front of me. Too much exposure for the male eyes. I would do my best to bounce my eyes by jerking my head upward. The danger was pulled muscles in the neck. God help men to bounce their eyes, and God help women to dress modestly.

5. Use the blood of Jesus to blow out sexual temptations because of the lust of the eyes. The blood of Jesus is God's atomic bomb to blow out the fiery darts of sexual temptations. I am a blood breather: breathe in the blood and breathe out sin and temptation I use the blood of Jesus to cleanse me from all unrighteousness.
6. No close friendships with the opposite sex or closed doors with opposite sex in pastoral counseling or in friendships.
7. Enjoy the wife of your youth. "*Let thy fountain be blessed: and rejoice with the wife of thy youth. Let her be as the loving hind and pleasant roe; let her breasts satisfy thee at all times; and* ***be thou ravished always*** *with her love"* (Proverbs 5:18-19).

Chapter Nine

The Pillar of Resolving Marriage Conflicts

This pillar that I am writing on is not all original. Over my forty-eight years of ministry and being mentored by three outstanding spiritual fathers, many of these thoughts and principles have been down loaded into my heart and mind. I don't really know who to give credit and how many principles I am quoting that was learned from one of my mentors.

As I write this March 30, 2016, Marvelous Mary and I have been in a covenant marriage for fifty-seven years. We have been through many storms and setbacks. By the grace and wisdom of God we have been through many personal marriage conflicts and are still deeply in love.

Some of our conflicts in our marriage came because of my high expectations. During the early years of our marriage, I had an idea of what I wanted Mary to be like as my marriage mate. I discovered that I assumed certain actions from her because of an expectation that was born in my mind. Whenever she did not come through, it became a source of frustration and conflict. Mary had a few high expectations of me. She wanted me to be her fix it man, plant flower beds, keep a clean garage, keep a clean office, and never lose my temper. When her expectations didn't happen, *"Hope deferred makes the heart sick..."* (Proverbs 13:12).

When Mary said I do, I had certain expectations of her. At night, I expected a hot meal, and hot lips. Especially after the children came, there were not many hot meals and most often tired lips. I often tried to fix her. I tried to make her a hot tamale. One day, in her frustration, she made two requests of me: 1. "You knew what you got when you married me. Please quit trying to fix me"; 2. "Rod, let God fix me!" In other words, lower your expectations of me. Stop being disappointed and offended. Love me for who I am. That was over thirty years ago. I honored her request and our marriage conflicts have been few and far apart.

Another source of marriage conflict is the lack of knowing your role. As a husband to Mary, I am commanded to be her head: to be her provider and her protector. I am commanded to honor her as the weaker vessel: to love her and to serve her; to be the chief disciplinarian; to manage the home and to keep it in order; to pray for her and pray with her! Remember in chapter one, Marvelous and I got into a serious marriage conflict over birth control. I was anti-birth control; having five children she became an avid believer of birth control. The conflict went on for two or three years that began to move into a crisis. At crisis, we sought a third party to settle or resolve our personal conflict. We went to one of my spiritual fathers, Apostle Jim Clark. In wisdom, he gave us two biblical viewpoints. First to Mary, "Wives submit to your husbands as unto the Lord!" Then he gave me this word of wisdom, "Honor the weaker vessel." I made a decision to honor the weaker vessel and our conflict ended.

Mary's role is very clear in the word of God and she does well. God called her to be my help meet; to complete me. She is my cheerleader; she is my ready lover. She reverences me, and respects me as her head. She tenderly follows my lead as unto the Lord. She sweetly submits to me in final decisions but always give me her insight in a godly manner. As we live out our roles, marriage conflicts are at a minimum and most of the time, my home is filled with joy and peace.

In some marriages, a source of conflict is outside relationships. This was never a source of conflict in my marriage. As a pastor, I helped maneuver couples through these waters of conflicts caused by outside relationships. It can be in-laws. A demanding father-in-law or an over bearing mother-in-law who intervenes and manipulates a daughter or son can cause conflict in a marriage. I have counseled more than one marriage conflict because of a blended family. One-half of America is blended-families because of the epidemic of divorce resulting in children from both ex-mates. So often there is a spaghetti of conflicts in second and third marriages: custody arrangements; financial pressure; this is my child and your child attitudes. A wife in a blended family conflict will often state, “You treat your child better than my child!” It needs to be the covenant language of our children. For a marriage to survive a blended family conflict, there must be a defining of roles and expectations. There cannot be a parent who is an enabler with a rebellious child. There must be a daily yielding to the Holy Spirit and a continual attitude of forgiveness!

Four truths that help in resolving conflicts

First truth: **People tend to hate conflicts and usually run from it rather than deal with it.** I have heard it said, “Marriage is the school of character!” God uses relationship conflicts to cause brokenness and change your character as you repent and yield to the Holy Spirit.

I wrote a book, *Going Through The Storms of Life,* and shared a parable of the birds in regards to the winds of a storm. The ostrich doesn’t face the storm. Rather he sticks his head in the ground hoping the storm will just pass. The winds of the storm come and throw him over and it breaks his neck. In a marriage conflict, if you don’t face the storm, the winds of your differences and pressures will divide and destroy. Not the eagle, when the storms come, he flies to the cliff of a rock and faces the storm. When the winds begin to blow, he dives into the winds and mounts his wings. What came to destroy him, elevates him above the storm! In a marriage conflict, you must face the storm and work out your differences and because of it, you become an eagle, a victor rather that victim.

The second truth help in resolving a marriage conflict:

Because of character flaws in our self and our spouse, all of our marriages are going to have relationship conflicts. There are seasons when your home will be a burning furnace. One evening upon returning from work, my wife was at the door having a personal conflict with three small children who had worn her out with childhood squabbles and resistance. It was an open furnace of conflict and confusion. I sat my three down, I faced my storm, and I told them that's my wife that you are dealing with. Their eyes widened in fear and I firmly spanked and prayed with them. Character flaws were dealt with and there was peace in my home and in my marriage.

The third truth help in resolving relationship conflict: **If you don't resolve a personal conflict, the relationship will move into a crisis**. If the crisis is not settled, there will be a disruption in the relationship. Often, in a marriage, it will result in a separation and eventually a divorce. Especially for a woman, she cannot exist emotionally under an angry or abusive husband. Again, an unresolved conflict and crisis will bring termination to a relationship.

The fourth truth in resolving conflict: **God wants your conflict or crisis to turn into covenant**. Covenant is a divine resolution of all difference and hostility. Over my forty-six years of ministry, I have seen more than a few marriages in crisis and seemingly hopeless turn into covenant: Homes and relationships of peace and joy. With this thought in mind, let's consider four steps in resolving personal conflicts.

> *"Recompense to no man evil for evil. Provide things honest in the sight of all men.* 18 *If it be*

possible, as much as lieth in you, live peaceably with all men." (Romans 12:17-18)

1. **First Step – Take the initiative.**

"Be ye angry, and sin not: let not the sun go down upon your wrath: [27] neither give place to the devil." (Ephesians 4:26-27)

Obey the word, don't let the sun go down on your anger and conflict. Don't give the devil jurisdiction to divide and destroy your marriage or any other personal relationship. As I wrote earlier, you must face your conflict. You must not fear dealing with conflict. In fear, you become defensive and distant. "I just don't want to deal with it!" Don't push your conflict under the rug: time will not heal it. The longer the conflict is unresolved the worse it will get. Rather, get the courage of God and work through your conflict. In over the fifty-seven years of my marriage, we have had our share of differences and conflicts. I thank God for a wife who would not allow our conflicts to remain unresolved. Often, she took the initiative to confront me and deal with our differences until they were settled.

2. **Second Step – Consider the right place.**

Marvelous Mary and I never discussed our differences of conflicts in a public place or before our children. My five children may have noticed some disagreements but they never heard an argument or saw strife and anger between Mary and I. Therefore, they were raised in a home of security, peace, and a sense of well-being.

3. **Third Step – Plan a right time in a private place**.

Mary never confronted me with a conflict when I came in from work unless it was an issue with our children. We tried to discuss our disagreements at a relaxed time. Over the years, we learned to listen to each other, rather than trying to win the argument. At a planned meeting, we most often came up with a positive attitude and agreement not with attacks or demands.

> *"There is that speaketh like the piercings of a sword: but the tongue of the wise is health."* (Proverbs 12:18)

Focus on reconciliation, not resolution. Resolution is to resolve all the issues and the differences. In some cases, resolution may never happen.

Another principle I learned in regards to overcoming conflicts. This thought was shared by Stephen Aguillard, my son who is a pastor. He and his wife taught, "In your marriages celebrate your differences." Therefore, I concluded, "Esteem your relationships more than your differences!"

One example of practicing this truth happened following one of Mary's shopping experiences. Of course, she went to her favorite bargain store, T.J. Maxx. She came home with her prize with excitement showing me a new dress. With a lady shoppers joy she shared, “It was retailed for $90.00 and I only paid $30.00 for it. I saved you $60.00.” My response, “You saved me $60.00. Where is it? I want to put it in our savings account.” She was baffled by my logical response. She said, “No! No! You do not understand, it was $90.00, I bought it for $30.00; I saved you $60.00.” My very logical and truthful response was “No, you did not save me $60.00 you spent $30.00.” To say the least, this was a very awkward exchange which could have caused a brief conflict in our marriage relationship. But, we smiled and we celebrated our differences. C’mon you can do it, “Esteem your relationship more than your differences! Celebrate your differences!”

4. The fourth step in resolving personal or marriage conflicts: **Confess your part of that which is causing the conflict**. This is not easy for proud men. In every marriage conflict, it takes two to fight. Mary may be ninety percent wrong and I may only be ten percent wrong. But I must deal with my ten percent responsibility in resolving the conflict or being reconciled. This is a truth. Most relationships die because of one or both being inflexible. Too egotistical or to self-centered rather than other centered. A proud stand, I am unwilling to move or to be vulnerable: “I may not always be right but I am never wrong.”

Mary and I have broken relational log jams on many occasions during our fifty-seven years of marriage. Someone decided to be humble and make the first move. One or both said, “I am sorry!” Someone listened and said, “I understand!” Log jam broken!

Three confessions of humility, 1. “I was wrong!” 2. “I am sorry!” 3. “I need help!” (Ron Corzine).

CHAPTER TEN

The Pillar of Romance for an Amazing Marriage

Romance involves a love pursuit between a man and woman. The Webster defines romance as carrying on a love affair between a man and a woman; to try to influence or carry favor with another person by lavishing personal attention, gifts, and compliments. Romance means to give special attention to someone of the opposite sex in order to develop a romantic relationship. To be romantic is to be marked by expressions of love or affection. It is to think about love and do and say things to that special someone to show that you have deep interest in beginning a courtship.

I was a freshman in college when I first laid eyes on my wife, Marvelous Mary. She was a freshman in high school and was matured way beyond her years. I was sitting in a football stadium with a shaved head and my big ears in full show. I had a duck caller tied around my neck. She happened to look up in the stands and our eyes met and an obvious interest of a romantic relationship began. I later said on her part it was love and first sight. She has stated, "Not so, I was a gold digger. I thought you were from a wealthy family." I saw beauty and she saw money. What a great beginning!

Later, the young men couldn't understand it. How did I attract and eventually become her steady boyfriend. She was certainly the green-eyed, shapely beauty of Eunice High School in Eunice, Louisiana. Their conclusion was "Lucky Lips!" Later after we were married, she did express admiration for my lips calling them beautiful. So the young men may have been partially right, "Lucky Lips!"

In romantic relationships, a man in love will always express admiration for his lady's physical and personality attributes. Listen to King Solomon's admiration for his lover:

> *"Behold, thou art fair my love...you are beautiful..."* (Song of Solomon 4:1)

Husbands, tell your wife often that she is beautiful. If you want honey give honey. If you want to fuel the romance in your marriage, admire her physical beauty. Marvelous Mary is seventy-two years old and she is beautiful. I tell her often and she purrs like a female cat!

Then King Solomon continues his romantic quest with words of admiration:

> *"you have dove eyes within your locks, (you have beady eyes)."* (Solomon 4:1)

Rather than beady, he must have meant soft eyes. Marvelous Mary has gorgeous green eyes; they sparkle like diamonds in the dew. She is the Cajun yellow rose of Louisiana. I love to romance her. As I do, her eyes smile at me and give me the bedroom look. Not bad for a couple in their seventies.

Solomon goes on with his romantic compliments.

> *"Your hair is as a flock of goats...your teeth like a flock of sheep that are even shorn which came up from the washing..."* (Song of Solomon 4:1-2)

Strange statements of admiring his lover's physical structure. But do compliment your wife's hair, it is her glory! It shines for you. Teeth like sheep must mean very white and 'even shorn' must mean they were well shaped. If your wife has beautiful teeth tell her. If she doesn't remain quiet. Any criticism of her physical make up will deflate romance.

Not to bore you, I am going to quote Song of Solomon 4:5,

> *Thy breasts are like two twin fawns...feeding among the lilies..."*

This means the breast are obvious and twins mean they are shaped alike. Men, it is not an evil thing to admire and compliment your wife's breast. Tell her how beautiful and shapely her breasts are. In fact, the Word of God encourages the following as part of your romantic marriage relationship.

"Let her be as the loving hind and pleasant roe; let her breasts satisfy thee at all times; and be thou ravished always with her love." (Proverbs 5:19)

This is one of my favorite scriptures in the Bible. Whenever my wife has a weak moment and accuses me of being too caught up in this particular part of her body structure, I refer her to this truth!

Men, in roles of marriage, God has appointed you not only to be the head of your home but to be the aggressor by adoring and cherishing her. There are at least four ways that I have learned to adore and cherish Marvelous Mary.

1. **I have learned her love language**. Her love language is not touch and it is not gifts. Her love language is service. I am not a skilled handyman. But I can do unskilled acts of service. I deposit love in her bank when I dig holes in the yard for her plants. At least once a month, we take a weekend break from our ministry travels. On that particular Sunday Mary is awake at 5:00 AM to cook for at least two family couples that include grandsons and granddaughters plus other special guests. Usually the number is between twenty and twenty-five hungry individuals. On occasion, after the feeding, I help her clean up the pots and pans. By doing so I am adoring and cherishing her. A romantic atmosphere is being borne in her heart. My wife related a humorous illustration to me of a woman's response to a romantic tip: "Sex begins in the kitchen for a married couple." She

misunderstood and gave this response to that word of wisdom "I could never have sex in the kitchen, we have too many windows."

2. **From my heart, I compliment her**. I adore her with positive words. By the way, a compliment a day will keep the devil away. Listed are a few compliments: "You are beautiful!" – "You are my woman!" – "You are wonderful!" – "You are a great mother and grandmother!" – "You are a great cook!" The Bible teaches that the power of life and death is in our words. Our words are containers, they either contain acceptance and affirmation or rejection. Harsh words release rejection into a person's mind. Gentle words, affirming words release life and acceptance into your spouse's mind and heart. The fires of romance burn in response.

Too often a husband will miss the mark with his demands and commands short circuiting a romantic relationship with his wife. The caveman or macho man persona is anti-romantic. In the evening, when you walk in the home from work, it is not romantic to demand a hot dinner, hot coffee, and hot lips.

3. **Thirdly, in my marriage by the grace of God**: **I endeavor to maintain an attitude of gratitude.** Men, as the leader in your marriage relationship, the Holy Spirit expects you to fuel the romance. Gratitude is ninety-eight percent octane gasoline to fire up the engine of a romantic relationship. First of all thank her for who she is! Listen to the wisdom and gratitude expressed by the writer in Proverbs:

> *"A worthy woman who can find? For her price is far above rubies. [11] The heart of her husband trusteth in her, And he shall have no lack of gain. [12] She doeth him good and not evil, all the days of her life."* Proverbs 31:10-12 (ASV)

Often, I have expressed gratitude to Mary for her value to me, that I trust her with my life. More than once, I have told her that I don't deserve her. She is too good to me, her value is far about rubies.

> *"Her husband is known in the gates, When he sitteth among the elders of the land."* (Proverbs 31:23)

I am so grateful to Marvelous Mary. I am part of an apostolic team with some of the finest spiritual leaders in America, and she is a big part of who I am and I let her know the same. This is gratitude; it fuels the romantic feelings in her heart.

In a husband's attitude of gratitude, we thank our wives for all they do.

> *"She riseth also while it is yet night, And giveth food to her household, And their [a]task to her maidens."* (Proverbs 31:15)

Let's be real men, our wives are often up early seeing

about our household. Marvelous is up at 5:00 am on Sunday morning cooking for a herd of twenty-five family members. I remember when we had five children at home. She gave her time to care for them: shopped groceries, feed, bathed and clothed, washed and dried tons of clothes; flossed their teeth and (by the way, I don't recall a dental bill because of this virtuous mother).

> *"She is not afraid of the snow for her household;*
> *For all her household are clothed with scarlet."*
> (Proverbs 31:21)

I am so thankful for all that my wife has done and is doing. When she opens her mouth wisdom flows. And she is so kind!

> *"The law of kindness is on her tongue."* (Proverbs 31:26)

So we rise-up and praise her, and thank her.

> *"Her children rise up, and call her blessed; Her husband also, and he praiseth her..."* (Proverbs 31:28)

Holy Spirit help us to be thankful in all things. Help us not to take anything for granted. Help us to thank our wives in the little things as well as the big things. A very short example list of being thankful to your wife; fueling her romantic heart:

1. “Thank you for this meal. It is delicious!”

2. “Thank you for taking care of our home. The bathroom smells wonderful!”

3. “Thank you for feeding the dogs!”

4. “Thank you for keeping our bedroom neat!”

5. “Thank you for our love making time! You were great!”

4. **The fourth way that I have learned to adore and cherish Marvelous Mary is to date her**, give her quality time! When I was pastoring a local church, our date time was Friday night. We would farm out our children and take off for a night of fun, food and fellowship. I would dine her at her favorite restaurant, not McDonalds. On most occasions, she would enjoy shopping at TJ Max and Marshall’s and with patience. I endured this part of our romantic night. In the car we would hold hands and converse with each other but no mention of problems or the work of our ministry. Later, in the night in the privacy of our bedroom we would make love! Men, if you want honey, give honey. Date and woo her once a week. This leads to the ultimate human communication of a marriage relationship: sex in the marital bedroom! If you follow my advice on all the previous thoughts in adoring and cherishing; you will have a wonderful romantic life with your wife. Let’s spend a few pages on describing it.

God’s word declares that He gave the gift of sex for **procreation and pleasure**.

"And God blessed them, and God said unto them, be fruitful, and multiply, and replenish the earth, and subdue it: and have dominion over the fish of the sea, and over the fowl of the air, and over every living thing that moveth upon the earth." (Genesis 1:28)

I have always said that when man separated procreation from pleasure, the birth control movement was birthed. Margaret Sanger, a witch from the East, was the promoter of birth control which evolved into Planned Parenthood which aborts 330,000 unborn babies a year and sells body parts. Her goal was to use birth control to eliminate the black race. She failed but birth control is now fully embraced by the body of Christ. The average family before birth control was seven children. It is now 1.8 children. We have disobeyed the mandate of Genesis 1:28 which was never canceled or withdrawn. It is still the Father's heart that the marriage bed reproduces multiple children.

In the beginning, God also gave the gift of sex for pleasure and intimate one on one intimacy. In the sex act, the married couple experience the ultimate of communication. It is a sacred act, where two separate human beings experiences a bonding of body, soul, and spirit. They truly become one. Therefore, it is not only glorious in pleasure but it is a sacred union that no outside person has the right to participate or share in. Whenever someone violates this sacred union, it is called adultery and it makes the marriage bed impure. If there is not serious repentance and the couple is brought through restoration, the marriage relationship will end.

God's word declares that He intended for sexual intimacy and intercourse to be a pleasure above all pleasures.

> *"Let your love and your sensual embrace with your wife intoxicate you continually with delight. Always enjoy the ecstasy of her love."* (Proverbs 5:18-19, paraphrased)

Intoxicate means to excite and please someone in a way that suggests the effect of alcohol or a drug; to excite or elate to the point of frenzy; exhilarate, thrill, titillate, turn-on. Ecstasy means a state of extreme delight; a state of overwhelming emotion or rapturous delights; cloud nine, euphoria, rapture, exhilaration, rhapsody, etc. These two terms, intoxicate and ecstasy, help to describe the sexual union of husband and wife.

Even in your older age, it still offers much pleasure; it's God's gift for the marriage bed. I was having trouble sleeping. A pastor friend of mine shared his secret of sweet sleep. He said to me "when you lay down at night, tell your feet to go to sleep; tell your legs to go to sleep; tell your hips and stomach to go to sleep; tell your chest and neck to go to sleep and you slumber off into a deep sleep." That night I tried it, "I told my feet to go to sleep; my legs to go to sleep; my hips and stomach to go to sleep (I was getting drowsy, as I told my chest and neck to go to sleep and as I was about out, my wife walked in with a thin negligee. I hit myself all over and I said everybody wake up; wake up." The anticipation of great sex in marriage wakes up a husband and a wife!

Listen to the lover of King Solomon 1:2-4.

> *"Let him kiss me with the kisses of his mouth: for thy love is better than wine. [3] Because of the savour of thy good ointments thy name is as ointment poured forth, therefore do the virgins love thee. [4] Draw me, we will run after thee: the king hath brought me into his chambers: we will be glad and rejoice in thee, we will remember thy love more than wine: the upright love thee."*

The following is a sex observation: a woman's number one needs is affection; to be adored and cherished for who she is. This turns her on! A man's number one need is reverence and running neck to neck with reverence is sex. Most men don't understand a wife's deep need for affection. The late Dr. Smalley said that a wife needs seven non sexual touches a day. That's not easy for a young husband. Over the years, a man grows into this level of affection and maturity.

Most women don't understand a husband's deep need for sex. By divine design, because of testosterone, he is the aggressive lover. That's why he grabs for you and paws on you and chases you around the bedroom. The average male reloads with testosterone within seventy-two hours after sexual intercourse. Some have a quicker reload.

By the way, for a wife/woman to aggressively express

romantic affection is not sin. The lover of King Solomon said,

> *"...we will run after thee; the king has brought me into his bed chambers..."* (Song of Solomon 1:4)

To bring it home, for a wife to say "Let's run to the bedroom!" is not weird. It seldom happens. In my marriage it never happened. But remember ladies, sensuality in the marriage bed is not sensual. Refuse the quit trips of past illicit sexual exploits. You are forgiven. Marvelous Mary, my wife, read a book called "Laugh Your Way into a Better Marriage" by Mark Gungor. From this great book she gleaned several health benefits of marital sex.

1. It relieves stress;
2. Lowers blood pressure;
3. Improves cardiovascular health;
4. Boosts self-esteem;
5. Reduces pain;
6. Reduces prostate cancer;
7. Helps you sleep better.

I read in another report, "Men who experience three or more orgasms a week reduce their heart attack risk by fifty percent." This is according to U.K. medical researchers.

So wives, let him have it as much as he wants. Better yet, as a couple return to your first love. When you were a young couple: you communicated daily; honored each other; date weekly and enjoy your sexuality. Closing advice, pray for one another on a daily basis, exercise often or stay in top physical shape for each other. Shower or bath often; smell good and look sharp for each other.

In closing, may you practice these ten pillars for an amazing marriage and enjoy the bliss of each other as Mary and I have for fifty-seven years. God Bless you! God strengthen you and yours in Jesus name!

RECOMMENDED READING

- *Love and Respect* by Dr. Emerson Eggerichs
- *Love Busters* by Willard F. Harley, Jr.
- *His Needs Her Needs* by William F. Harley, Jr.
- *The Five Love Languages* by Gary Chapman
- *Laugh Your Way to a Better Marriage* by Mark Gungor
- *Intimate Issues* by Linda Dillow and Lorraine Pintus
- *Sex Begins in the Kitchen* by Dr. Kevin Leman
- *Sheet Music* by Dr. Kevin Leman

The Good News:

God's plan for your forgiveness of sins and your entrance into Heaven.

1. Every human being is born with a sin nature and all of us sin. *"For all have sinned and fall short of the Glory of God..."* **Romans 3:23**

2. Therefore, all of us are sinners and all of us need a savior. The Good News: *"But God demonstrates His own love toward, in that while we were still sinners, Christ died for us."* **Romans 5:8**

3. Religion, rules, and rituals can't save you from your state of sin and death! Rather, you are invited to have a personal relationship with Jesus Christ. The Good News: *"For the wages of sin is death but the gift of God is eternal life in Christ Jesus our Lord."* **Romans 6:23**

4. Right now...Repent of your sins and turn from your selfishness. Call out to Jesus Christ to be your Lord and Savior. *"...if you confess with your mouth the Lord Jesus and believe in your heart that God raised him from the dead, you will be saved."* **Romans 10:9**

The meaning of being saved: By grace and faith in the redeeming blood of Jesus, a man is delivered from the power of sin, Satan and selfishness into the life of grace, peace and righteousness.

everybody wake up; wake up." The anticipation of great sex in marriage wakes up a husband and a wife!

Listen to the lover of King Solomon 1:2-4.

> *"Let him kiss me with the kisses of his mouth: for thy love is better than wine. [3] Because of the savour of thy good ointments thy name is as ointment poured forth, therefore do the virgins love thee. [4] Draw me, we will run after thee: the king hath brought me into his chambers: we will be glad and rejoice in thee, we will remember thy love more than wine: the upright love thee."*

The following is a sex observation: a woman's number one needs is affection; to be adored and cherished for who she is. This turns her on! A man's number one need is reverence and running neck to neck with reverence is sex. Most men don't understand a wife's deep need for affection. The late Dr. Smalley said that a wife needs seven non sexual touches a day. That's not easy for a young husband. Over the years, a man grows into this level of affection and maturity.

Most women don't understand a husband's deep need for sex. By divine design, because of testosterone, he is the aggressive lover. That's why he grabs for you and paws on you and chases you around the bedroom. The average male reloads with testosterone within seventy-two hours after sexual intercourse. Some have a quicker reload.

By the way, for a wife/woman to aggressively express

romantic affection is not sin. The lover of King Solomon said,

> *"...we will run after thee; the king has brought me into his bed chambers..."* (Song of Solomon 1:4)

To bring it home, for a wife to say "Let's run to the bedroom!" is not weird. It seldom happens. In my marriage it never happened. But remember ladies, sensuality in the marriage bed is not sensual. Refuse the quit trips of past illicit sexual exploits. You are forgiven. Marvelous Mary, my wife, read a book called "Laugh Your Way into a Better Marriage" by Mark Gungor. From this great book she gleaned several health benefits of marital sex.

1. It relieves stress;
2. Lowers blood pressure;
3. Improves cardiovascular health;
4. Boosts self-esteem;
5. Reduces pain;
6. Reduces prostate cancer;
7. Helps you sleep better.

I read in another report, "Men who experience three or more orgasms a week reduce their heart attack risk by fifty percent." This is according to U.K. medical researchers.

So wives, let him have it as much as he wants. Better yet, as a couple return to your first love. When you were a young couple: you communicated daily; honored each other; date weekly and enjoy your sexuality. Closing advice, pray

The Good News:

God's plan for your forgiveness of sins and your entrance into Heaven.

1. Every human being is born with a sin nature and all of us sin. *"For all have sinned and fall short of the Glory of God..."* **Romans 3:23**

2. Therefore, all of us are sinners and all of us need a savior. The Good News: *"But God demonstrates His own love toward, in that while we were still sinners, Christ died for us."* **Romans 5:8**

3. Religion, rules, and rituals can't save you from your state of sin and death! Rather, you are invited to have a personal relationship with Jesus Christ. The Good News: *"For the wages of sin is death but the gift of God is eternal life in Christ Jesus our Lord."* **Romans 6:23**

4. Right now...Repent of your sins and turn from your selfishness. Call out to Jesus Christ to be your Lord and Savior. *"...if you confess with your mouth the Lord Jesus and believe in your heart that God raised him from the dead, you will be saved."* **Romans 10:9**

The meaning of being saved: By grace and faith in the redeeming blood of Jesus, a man is delivered from the power of sin, Satan and selfishness into the life of grace, peace and righteousness.

Need
Additional
Copies?

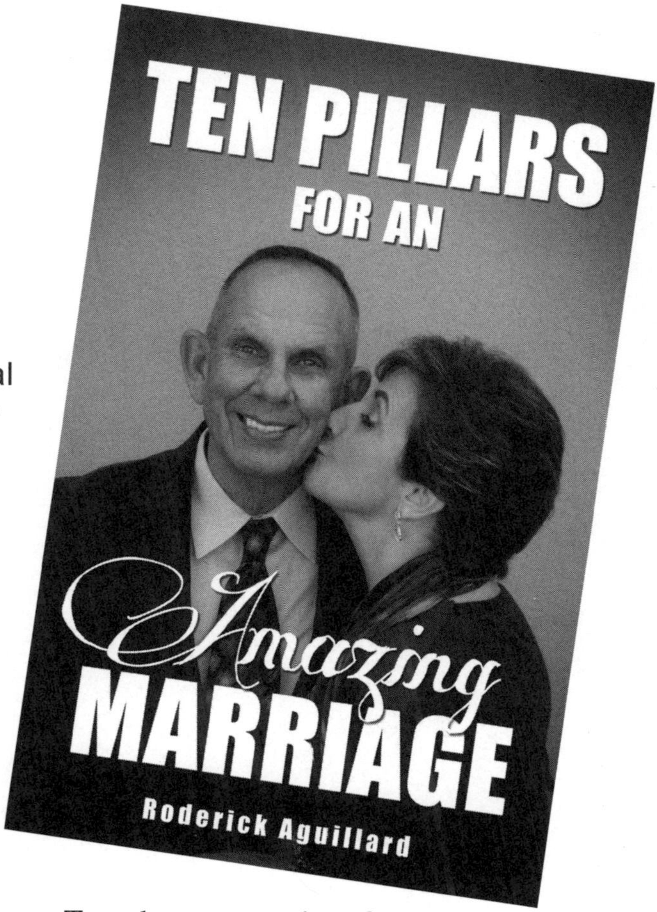

To order more copies of

TEN PILLARS FOR AN *Amazing* MARRIAGE

contact CertaPublishing.com

- ❒ Order online at CertaPublishing.com/TenPillarsforanAmazingMarriage
- ❒ Call 855-77-CERTA
- ❒ Email Info@CertaPublishing.com or
- ❒ Email Info@NRPastors.com

Certa PUBLISHING